Vicky,

May I be of

be used of the Lord as you read

the message the Lord has led me

to share.

Tapestry in the Master's Hands

Naomi R. Jantz

The blessings God sends to us are diamonds which are priceless; they are disguised as difficulties and interruptions. God uses them to weave the tapestry of our lives.

Naomi R Jantz

WESTBOW
PRESS
A DIVISION OF THOMAS NELSON
& ZONDERVAN

Taken from My Utmost for His Highest® by Oswald Chambers, edited by James Reimann, © 1992 by Oswald Chambers Publications Assn., Ltd., and used by permission of Discovery House Publishers, Grand Rapids MI 4950l. All rights reserved.

Scripture taken from the Holy Bible, NEW INTERNATIONAL VERSION®. Copyright © 1973, 1978, 1984 by Biblica, Inc. All rights reserved worldwide. Used by permission. NEW INTERNATIONAL VERSION® and NIV® are registered trademarks of Biblica, Inc. Use of either trademark for the offering of goods or services requires the prior written consent of Biblica US, Inc.

WestBow Press books may be ordered through booksellers or by contacting:

WestBow Press
A Division of Thomas Nelson & Zondervan
1663 Liberty Drive
Bloomington, IN 47403
www.westbowpress.com
1 (866) 928-1240

ISBN: 978-1-4908-7167-7 (sc)
ISBN: 978-1-4908-7166-0 (hc)
ISBN: 978-1-4908-7181-3 (e)

Library of Congress Control Number: 2015903314

Print information available on the last page.

WestBow Press rev. date: 4/27/2015

I wrote in my journal on September 14, 1986, "Maybe someday I will write a book," and you, dear reader, are now holding that dream in your hands. May God speak to you as you read *Tapestry in the Master's Hands.*

Some of the names in the book have been changed to protect individual privacy, and I have also added some permission-granted humor.

Acknowledgments

Gary Moore, thank you for believing in me and encouraging me to write my story. Without you, my dream would not have become a reality.

Dave Stephens, thank you for not running the other way when I approached you for help. I am grateful for your help in making my writing dreams come true. You have done a superb job!

Deanna, Denise, and Charlene, my beautiful daughters, God blessed your daddy and me with three amazing girls. Thank you for your encouragement and support during this writing process. You believed in my vision that my story would be published.

Thank you to the team at WestBow Press, who published Orlando's and my story. You have been extremely kind and helpful.

Josh Roesener Photography, thanks for your superb work with the images in my book.

Most important, I give thanks to my heavenly Father. I am grateful for the individuals He has sent across my path to bring my story to my family, my friends, and the world. Thank You, Jesus, for making this journey a colorful one.

Bob Gass, Author The Word For You Today Alpharetta, Georgia

To my valentine, Orlando, who reflected God's love in every way. All who knew you felt your giving heart, your gentle spirit, and your sacrificial love. You were a marvelous companion and friend for fifty-three years. You brought much happiness to my life, and we enjoyed being a team through fifty years of ministry. I am forever grateful for your love.

And to my wonderful children, Deanna, Denise, and Charlene, for always being affirmers and encouragers during my writing journey. You are constant reminders of the godly heritage left to you by your awesome daddy. I see him in each of you every day.

Contents

CHAPTER 1

Christmas Eve

It was Christmas Eve 2011. Outside, the snowflakes fell lazily to the ground. We had just come in from a hayrack ride in the pasture on the family farm. Our cheeks were kissed with the beautiful icy flakes of snow. No Christmas for our family had ever been complete until we took a hayrack ride while singing Christmas carols. A cup of hot chocolate with marshmallows floating on top after coming in from the cold would be the next item on the agenda. Orlando had always driven the tractor pulling the hay wagon, lately with our six grandchildren, along with other family members, but he had passed away on May 24 of that year.

"Grandma," said my oldest grandson, Joshua, as we sat in the parlor drinking our hot chocolate, "tell us the story of your life." My grandsons Coby and Luke called me *Ma,* while the other boys—Joshua, Brady, Earl Ray, and Trevor—called me *Grandma.* The boys all chimed in with "Please, Ma!"

I looked around at my grandchildren, who were sitting in a circle around my rocker, big smiles on their faces. Six pairs of eyes looked at me with anticipation.

But where, I wondered, *do I begin?* I had never told my whole life story before, and a lifetime was not a simple thing. It is complex, like the weaving of a tapestry, with each day another thread woven to the next by a great and awesome God. Did my story start with my birth? What about the events that led to it? What about those who came before me, the ancestors who followed God's call long before my own parents were born?

"Well," I said, "the only place my story can begin is on the other side of the world, long before I was born."

CHAPTER 2

By Sea, Air, and Boxcar

It all began many years ago when my grandpa, Gerhard F. Kornelsen, emigrated from the village of Hoffnungsburg in the Crimea of South Russia with his parents, Gerhard E. and Aganetha Kornelsen, when he was six years old. The family arrived in New York on the ship *S. S. Cimbria* on August 27, 1874. During the voyage Grandpa Gerhard—who, you remember, was just a little boy and who had an affinity for the unusual— became enamored of the round porthole and wondered what was on the other side. His head just fit the opening, and there was considerable difficulty in pulling his head back. He decided that sticking one's head in it was not the way to investigate the unknown.

Four years later, on July 2, 1878, my grandma, Elizabeth Schierling, who was later to be Gerhard's wife, landed in New York, immigrating with her parents, Wilhelm and Anna Schierling. They came from the village of Fuerstenwerder in the Molotschna Colony, South Russia, on the ship *S. S. Strassburg*. Both families came to America seeking religious freedom.

My great-grandpa Kornelsen finally settled in Inman, Kansas, with his family. Just as an exquisite quilt is woven, so lives intertwine, and Wilhelm and Anna Schierling and their family also eventually settled in Inman, Kansas.

Life was hard for farmers in those days, but weathering many difficulties and depending on their strong faith in God, they raised crops to make a living. Their food came from vegetable gardens, cows provided them with milk, and meat came from their cattle and the game they hunted. Ingenuity was required to survive! My grandpa Kornelsen became acquainted with the attractive teenager, Elizabeth Schierling, and used his shiny two-wheeled buggy to visit her. After a romantic courtship, they were married on October 1, 1891.

They made their home west of Inman on a farm owned by my grandpa Kornelsen's father. They lived in a humble one-room sod house, where eight children were born, one of whom was my father, William, better known as "Willie."

In 1904, the family moved from the one-room sod house to a thirteen-room house, better known as the "big house." It was the first home in the area to have a central furnace system. One other feature of the house was a wrap-around porch that many neighborhood children and, later, grandchildren enjoyed using to play hide-and-seek.

In about 1937, a plane flown by Bud Potter experienced engine failure over Grandpa Gerhard's, farm, and Potter had to make a "dead stick" landing. Grandpa helped Bud repair the plane, and when it was ready to fly again, took a ride in Potter's open-cockpit plane. From that point on, Grandpa was hooked on the thrill of flying, and at the age of 72, he purchased a Cessna 120. He hired a pilot—none other than Bud Potter—and later purchased a Cessna 170 and enjoyed the larger plane for many years. He loved his years of flying; he could never get enough of it.

During the prime years of Grandpa Gerhard's life, he worked to ensure that each of his children had a farm. This desire to provide for his children led to his purchase of two farms around the Inman area. When farmland became too expensive in that area, he went on a land-buying expedition in western Kansas and bought additional farms for his other children. Then he owned eight farms: one for each of his seven living children and one for himself.

Grandpa took his last flight, the most glorious he had ever taken, on June 26, 1950. At the age of eighty-two, after suffering a stroke, he took his final flight on angel wings that lifted him to his eternal, heavenly home.

After a pause, I said to my grandsons, "Hey, boys, when you want to save money, where do you put it?"

"In the bank," they responded in unison.

"I'm sure that's where we would put it, but not my grandpa."

"Where did he put it?" Coby asked.

"In a metal pipe!" I replied.

Following his funeral, the tools in his two-story woodshop were divided among his children. The pipe was lying in an unusual spot, which led one of his sons to investigate. When he moved the pipe, silver dollars rolled out all over the concrete floor. Of course, the excitement of finding Grandpa's secret financial hiding place did not compensate for the grief his family was feeling.

In 1924, while attending school at Zoar Academy in Inman, my father, William "Willie" Kornelsen, met a charming young lady named Elsie Unruh, who was from Pawnee Rock, Kansas. During the summers, the desire to court Elsie was stronger than the inconvenience of the lack of money for travel, so Willie would hop on one of a train's boxcars, hang on for dear life, and make his way to Pawnee Rock, a trip of more than seventy-five miles.

Willie was a determined man, and when his mind was made up, he achieved what he desired. On March 21, 1926, Willie and Elsie were married in the K.M.B. Church near Greensburg, Kansas. They remembered the wonderful day as an exciting one in part because nature crowned the day with a deluge of rain.

Her groom told Elsie that he had planned a mysterious honeymoon, so she waited with anticipation to see what was in store for her. When the mystery was revealed, Elsie realized Willie was a man of action and surprises, as he couldn't wait until a home was built and ready for his beautiful bride, so he took Elsie immediately to the farm his father had homesteaded six miles north and a quarter mile east of Minneola, Kansas. The mode of transportation was a uniquely decorated buggy pulled by Willie's favorite horse. The newly married couple spent the first few nights of their honeymoon under the twinkling stars with the night sounds of chirping crickets lulling them to sleep. It took Willie two months to build a one-room shed where they could live. He carried his bride over the threshold of her new home, and Elsie set up housekeeping.

That year, Kansas was experiencing a drought, so Willie knew it would be difficult to get a crop to start growing. Being ingenious, he planted wheat seeds in soil in gunnysacks. He kept the gunny sacks watered, and when the seeds sprouted, he excitedly transferred his "gunny sack wheat crop" to the field. Willie eventually planted 280 acres of wheat with the help of the horse that had pulled their honeymoon buggy to the farm. Because one horse wasn't enough to take care of the work that had to be done, he bought another horse. Willie gave Grandpa Gerhard a third of the wheat crop; he had become a successful farmer.

Even though the horses were soon replaced with a Case tractor, Willie still used horses to help hoist cement for the purpose of building a storage tank for water. Soon a barn was built, and the newly married couple moved into the barn loft, leaving the one-room shed to serve as a chicken coop. Elsie had to carry water up to the loft using a ladder that leaned against the side of the barn. They shared their meager home with bales of hay stored there for cattle feed.

Willie started a cowherd on the two hundred acres of pasture grass that was part of the farm. Every day he threw hay down through an opening in the floor of their humble home, climbed down the ladder, and milked the cows. Talk about fresh milk! Cows, hay, and a young married couple: imagine the atmosphere, smells, and sounds. It was, to say the least, a humble beginning, but at least they weren't living in the chicken coop.

Their humble circumstances caught the attention of a pastor in Hutchinson, Kansas, who wrote about it in a devotional magazine in 2001:

> I am sure Willie and Elsie must have felt like Mary and Joseph. In Bethlehem, Jesus was born in a stable, barn, or a stall for livestock, perhaps nestled in a cave. His first crib was a feeding trough. It was not exactly a place suitable for royalty. It was not where monarchs would likely be found. It was as "down to earth" as you could get. It was, however, where the Son of God humbly began His fleshly existence. Talk about humble beginnings! Willie and Elsie began their life together humbly and simply. Willie and Elsie felt their humble "hay loft home" was crowned with the Royal Presence of their heavenly Father.

The cows were used for milk, but they also became Willie's pets. In fact, it wasn't unusual for Elsie to see her husband riding one of them out in the pasture. She tried to persuade him that this wasn't safe, and much to Willie's dismay, the habit was soon forfeited when he fell off of one of his "pets" and was badly hurt.

He raised calves and sold them when they reached approximately 800 pounds. When necessary, he kept one of the calves and grain-fed it to provide meat for the next year. A garden provided vegetables for Elsie to can and store in a cellar for the winter months. The couple also used this cellar as a storm shelter when there was a tornado threat, which was often, especially in the summer. Meals were prepared outdoors on an open fire pit. Willie thought Elsie was a gourmet cook, even though sometimes he was served burned chicken, fried on the outdoor fire, after a day of hard work in the field.

After living in the barn loft for some time, Willie felt it was time to update their living quarters. He purchased a kit home from the Sears Roebuck and Co. catalog and erected a two-room home.

After carrying water for so long, Elsie enjoyed pumping water for drinking, cooking, and washing from a hydrant in the home. Instead of preparing meals outside, she took delight in cooking on a stove, even if it was a challenge to control the heat on the stove, as the burners were fueled by kerosene.

Willie and Elsie were thrilled when their son Willard was born on June 19, 1929, but when the midwife was unable to clear Willard's air passage to keep him breathing, they desperately tried to reach a doctor. The doctor, who lived a considerable distance away, did not arrive in time, and Willie and Elsie's dream for a child faded away when Willard was only a few hours old. Even though they were in deep grief, life had to continue, and farming needed to be done if they were to survive physically and financially.

My mother and daddy knew it would be hard work working the farm, but little did they know the difficulties they would experience. The economy took a dive downward in the 1930s, when the Great Depression occurred, which included the Dust Bowl. They learned much about hard work, sacrifice, and sharing what they could with others—possibly a loaf or two of Elsie's marvelous homemade bread. By the sweat of their brows, faith in their heavenly Father to provide wisdom, and determination, they were able survive. Willie was purposeful and frugal and kept his perspective; when others were buying up more and more land, he took care of the acreage that had been given to him to the best of his ability by alternating his acres half into wheat and half into summer fallow, which allowed the soil to replenish itself. He walked the length and breadth of the land, digging out "bind weed" and other undesirables by hand.

"Willie, my great grandpa, must have been a unique man," Brady said.

"Yes, he was," I responded. "In fact, his pastor, the Reverend Stan Meek, shared his uniqueness in the Standard Sunday School paper of January 9, 2000:"

> This sturdy farmer of Russian ancestry had a ruddy face, textured by the sun and winds of the Plains. He loved the land, but he loved his Lord best of all, and he loved to pray. As one would peer intently across the golden heads of grain capped with shimmering beads of bright Kansas sunlight, one might even be able to detect the silhouette of a kneeling man beside that tractor. It was no mirage. The words of the song, "My God and I walk in the field together, we walk and talk as good friends should and do, we clasp our hands our voices ring with laughter, my God and I walk through the meadows hue," tell the story of Willie's lifestyle. Not long after I began pastoring in Dodge City, Willie pulled his pickup close to the parsonage door. As I stepped out to meet him, he rolled the window down, and with a boyish grin and a soft-spoken voice, he said, "Pastor, my wife and I want you and your family to come for dinner Sunday." I gratefully and eagerly accepted the invitation, and before he drove away, he drawled, "By the way, Pastor, we have a half a beef we want to give you if you can find room for it." Find room for it? Absolutely, we did! … For pastors, Sunday sermons keep coming like boxcars on an endless freight train. Willie, being big and strong and the outdoors type, yet tender enough to give me a hug each Sunday, would say, "That was a great message, Pastor." Willie was fantastic in the "Hug Department." When I received that special hug of his, I felt like I was snuggled right up next

to the heart of God. It's hard work building sermons, but a little appreciation creates miraculous, weekly sermon-building energy.

Rev. Meek went on to share that, periodically, as his wife Pat opened the parsonage door, one of Willie's family members was standing there with a freshly baked apple pie or homemade bread. What a fabulous way for Elsie to show love and appreciation for the pastor's family! Willie and Elsie knew how to be tremendous affirmers, Meek said, and went on to ask the question, "Was there some magic about Willie? No, the magic was not Willie at all. It was not even 'magic'; it was just *Jesus in Willie.*"

Elsie was a marvelous hostess to many. In fact, as guests sat around her table, she served a banquet fit for a king using whatever she had on hand, and made all feel welcome in my mother and daddy's home.

They loved the teens of the church, and many of them became their close friends. It wasn't unusual for a college student to receive a letter containing a small amount of money with a note saying, "This is for an ice-cream cone," or "use this for something that may be serendipity."

My mother and daddy shared with all who touched their lives a quality of fellowship that can only be characterized as true spiritual *koinonia*, or true, intimate fellowship. Their gratitude for life was not reserved just for the good times; when my daddy lay dying in the hospital with a tube down his throat and his mouth so very dry, he praised his Creator: "I've got my family, I have God, I have ice chips and a sip of water once an hour," Willie said. "I'm in luxury! I'm very content. All is in my heavenly Father's hands."

G. F. & Elizabeth (Schierling) Kornelsen

The Sod House
Home of G.F. and Elizabeth Kornelsen until the "Big" house was built.
All eight children were born in this house.

Grandpa G.F. Kornelsen and Bud Potter in front of G.F.'s airplane

William S. & Elsie (Unruh) Kornelsen

Tin shed—first home of Willie & Elise Kornelsen

CHAPTER 3

They named her
Naomi Ruth

Although, of course, I don't remember it, an exciting event took place on November 22, 1937, when, eight years after Willard died, a daughter was born in the two-room Sears & Roebuck home, and another thread was added to the tapestry they were helping to weave.

My parents already had a name picked out for their first daughter. That name, Naomi Ruth, became mine.

"Ma," my grandson Luke asked, "isn't that the name of someone in the Bible?"

"You're correct, Luke. In fact, it is the name of two women in the Old Testament: Ruth and her mother-in-law, Naomi."

When I was a year old, I was diagnosed with whooping cough, and for a while it looked like my mother and daddy were going to experience devastating sadness, just as they had eight years earlier. My parents felt it was a miracle that I recovered.

When I was two years old, I didn't have much hair, and my daddy shaved my head, hoping to help my hair grow in faster and thicker. My mother was so embarrassed that she wouldn't take me anywhere without a cap. Several years later, I had a full head of hair. Is that a great way to take care of baldness or what?

My parents enjoyed the thrill of my recovery from whooping cough for three years, but then my body became wracked with spinal meningitis. Because it was difficult to get a doctor to come quickly to the farm or to get me to a doctor, I almost died again, but with limited medical care and much prayer, your great grandma and grandpa again felt a miracle was given to them when I recovered from this difficult illness without any side effects.

We were hoping to have running water that we didn't have to pump, so my daddy had a well dug. I know it is fun to ride a horse, but horses can also be used for work. Because your great grandpa needed to save money, instead of hiring someone to build a supply tank to store water, he did the work himself, along with a few willing volunteers. He used horses to pull buckets of cement and poured it in wooden forms to build the tank to store the water. That tank was used for many years.

By this time, it was necessary to update the living quarters again, and my parents purchased a modular home and moved it to the farm. There was running water and my mother no longer had to prime a pump to get water into the kitchen. I also had my own bedroom—what fun! And even an inside bathroom! That was luxury! My daddy had built the outside bathroom to be quite fancy, with brick on the outside and a cement floor on the inside, and it was even a "two-seater," a pretty big deal, even then. As nice as it was, the inside bathroom was better.

Because your great grandma and grandpa were of German descent, we spoke German in our home. I spoke it fluently, but since my playmates couldn't understand what I was saying, my mother taught me to speak English. My mother and daddy spoke German at home all their lives but communicated in English outside the home.

With excitement, Coby spoke up: "Ma, please say something in German."

"*Ich liebe dich*," was my response. "That means 'I love you.'"

"Thanks. I love you too," Coby said.

"Did you teach any of your friends to speak German"? asked Trevor.

"I tried, but *meine Freunde*–that means 'my friends'—told me it was too difficult.

"Did your mother and daddy want to send you to a German school?" asked Brady.

"That wasn't possible since there wasn't one in the vicinity," I replied.

Minneola was the closet place for me to attend school. Since it was six miles from the farm, I rode the school bus. My first day of school was an adventure! One of my friends wanted me to come to her home to play, which sounded like fun to me. When it came time for me to arrive home after school and there was no Naomi on the bus, the bus driver told my parents that I hadn't gotten on the bus. You can imagine my mother's and daddy's concern. They immediately made a phone call to the principal, and he came looking for me.

"I assume that is the last time you enjoyed that type of adventure."
"You are correct, Earl Ray!"

My younger years seemed to be plagued with physical difficulties. When I was eight and in the third grade, I was diagnosed with "red measles" which turned into strep throat and rheumatic fever. My parents were told about a doctor in Dodge City, Kansas, who might be able to see me through this difficult time. After two weeks in the hospital, I was allowed to go home. Guess what, guys. Here I am, telling you my story, and I do not have any lasting effects from the rheumatic fever.

Since they had no son to help with outside responsibilities, I became my daddy's helper. Working outside was more exciting to me than doing household chores. I am proud to tell you that the reason you can go barefoot outside and not step on any stickers is that one of my chores was to go around this large yard and dig out those prickly weeds.

"Aren't you grateful?" I said, looking at each of my grandsons.
"You bet!" Luke said.
"How about mowing the yard?" asked Trevor. "You must have had a big lawn mower because it certainly is a huge yard!"
"Well, your great grandpa had a unique way of mowing.
"I'd like to know about that. Maybe it would make my lawn-mowing easier!" exclaimed Coby.
"You would need to put a fence around the yard and allow the cattle to eat the grass. You see, then you didn't need to rake the grass and put it in bags. My daddy thought it was a much easier way to mow, plus it gave the cattle some fresh food.

"What about picking up the cow chips?" asked Earl Ray.

"You are looking at the cow-chip picker-upper," I said with a smile.

"What were some of your other chores, Grandma?" asked Josh.

I milked cows, and many times, when I did, a kitty enjoyed milk squirted into her mouth. Sounds fun, don't you think?"

My mother ran the milk through a separator in the basement of our house to separate the milk from the cream. Then it would either be taken to town and sold or she would put the cream into a butter churn, and after it had aged sufficiently, turn the handle on the churn and make *real* butter. You talk about buying butter in the grocery store today, but not until you have had homemade butter do you know what *real* butter tastes like. There isn't anything that compares! Even now, I can smell homemade bread baking, and I remember waiting for it to finish baking so I could eat a slice with the fresh butter.

I gathered eggs from the chicken house, but sometimes the hens did not want me to get their eggs, so I had to reach under them quickly to get the eggs that were there. There were times I didn't reach quickly enough, and the hen would peck at my hand. *Ouch*! I also drove the truck during wheat harvest. Since my daddy didn't want to waste any time, it became my challenge to drive the wheat truck beside the combine without stopping as he unloaded the wheat. Your great grandpa had patience with me because, even though he didn't want any wheat spilled on the ground, there were times I couldn't stay close enough to the combine. Then I either took the grain to the co-op in Minneola or unloaded it at the farm, and the auger would put it into the storage silo. Guess what: the truck I drove was the same truck your grandpa used for harvest in June 2010.

Before you think my life was all work and no play, there were times my imagination kicked in and I walked in the shelter, the large belt of trees, pretending I was a pirate or a hunter looking for treasures that no one else could find. In the winter, with the protection of the trees, large banks of snow collected, and I pretended I was climbing up mountains and sliding down on the other side. Since I was an only child, my imaginary friend was a tremendous playmate. In the summer, I sat in the hayloft of the barn, where my mother and daddy had lived, with the aroma of the hay surrounding me. It was fun to hang my feet out the barn window and imagine I was on top of the world. It was a refreshing place to read a book!

"As you read books in the hayloft, you must have found some yummy recipes," said Coby. "You're a fantastic cook."

"I should have, but sad to say, those kinds of books didn't interest me. I liked to read mystery stories. I realized only later that, instead of spending time imagining and pretending, it would have been wise to learn how to cook!"

The summer I was twelve, a farmer's wife wanted me to work for her during harvest. My reaction? Absolutely! I needed some of those green things called dollars. Little did I know I would have to fry chicken, mashed potatoes and gravy, salad, and green beans for my first meal serving a harvest crew. How was I going to do it since I did not know how to cook? I had seen your great grandma doing it, so I decided I'd do what I thought my Mother would have done. No one got sick, and the harvest crew came back for the next meal. Maybe it was because they had been hungry and hadn't realized it had been cooked by someone who was cooking her first meal!

Since I had cooked for a harvest crew, I wanted to surprise my mother and daddy with a delicious meal. One day they went into town to buy groceries, which gave me the opportunity I had been waiting for. I had made fried chicken for a harvest crew, so I knew I could do it, but a new challenge was ahead of me: I first had to kill a rooster, singe off the feathers, and cut it up before I could fry it. I had seen my daddy kill a rooster and was positive I could do it. I got a board, caught the rooster, and held it by his feet. He squawked, but I finally got his head under the board. All I had to do then was stand on the board and yank, and his head should come off.

I yanked, but all the rooster did was squawk louder! I tried again. SQUAWK! After the third time, I felt sorry for him and let him go, but then he turned around and started chasing me. I ran for the house, my special surprise having turned into a disaster.

"Quit laughing, you guys, it wasn't funny, I was scared!" All of my grandsons were rolling around on the floor, howling with laughter.

Another one of my chores was to go into the pasture and turn the windmill on and off as necessary. My job on the way to the windmill was to search for any type of sticker weed, pull it, put it in a sack, and bring it back to the house to throw away. I kept not only the yard free of stickers but also the pasture. Your great grandpa was very particular about stickers. I enjoyed going to the windmill because it was a fun place to dream and pretend. I pretended I was a queen sitting on a throne and giving orders to all of my attendants or that I was a great singer. I sang at the top of my lungs, as there was no one to tell me any different except the cattle, and they thought I was tremendous! Sometimes they even chimed in with a "here a moo and there a moo." It was a super choir!

My daddy had cows to provide milk and steers to sell or provide meat, but he also had a large bull. When I was thirteen, I was seeking a teenage adventure and wanted to make friends with Buster, the bull. He seemed friendly enough when I was on the other side of the fence, so I crawled under the fence, walked over to where he was, and tried giving him some hay to eat. His friendliness did not last long: He pawed the ground, snorted, and acted as though I definitely was not a desirable companion. Instead of looking friendly, Buster now looked ferocious with his large horns and big black eyes. As I stood there holding my hay, I was so scared I could not move; my feet felt glued to the ground. Every time he pawed the ground with his hoof, my ears heard him say in his deep, gruff snort, "Here I come! Here I come!" I was finally able to pick up one foot and then the other and take off running to the fence. I crawled under the barbed-wire fence, tearing my shirt and scraping my arm in the process. I was just in time, because I could feel his breath on my skin as he stuck his head over the fence, snorting again as if to say, "Next time you won't be so lucky!

"You probably decided you never wanted that kind of adventure again," said Brady.

"You're right about that," I replied with a chuckle.

"Did you ever go back to the pasture?" asked Luke.

"Not until my daddy sold Buster!" I stood up and stretched. "Guys, don't you think it's time for another cup of hot chocolate?" I asked.

"Sounds great," they all chimed in, ready for a warm mug on a cold and snowy day, a day different from the one I was about to share with them. Instead of the beautiful snow sparkling like diamonds as we peered out the window, the day I was about to share was one of heartache and crises.

CHAPTER 4

Surviving the Storm, Making Music

Sometimes a dark thread that was not intended finds its way into a tapestry, but when the tapestry is finished, the weaver realizes the darker color has given it character and made it unique. God works in the same way by *allowing* a crisis to enter our lives. God uses it to build character and a good life, and like an intriguing story, a good life is full of charismatic characters.

It was April 1947, the day was beautiful, and I was playing outside with my friends. Then the weather changed, taking on an ominous feeling. The clouds turned black, and the air felt sticky and muggy. All became quiet, and the air smelled like rain. However, we were having so much fun that we did not realize that it was the perfect atmosphere for a tornado. My friends left when it was time for my mother and daddy and me to go to church in Dodge City.

While we were in church, we could hear the windows rattling and something pounding on the roof. This was before tornado-warning sirens, so the pastor dismissed church early.

The sixteen miles we had to drive to get home were difficult. I knew the storm was bad when we had to stop, not once but twice, to move large items off the highway and out of our way so we could pass. Even though it was hailing hard, my daddy got out of the car to move a telephone pole off the highway and then again to move a large piece of tin. I was becoming more frightened with each mile, but I had confidence my daddy would get us home safely.

When we turned off the highway and then into the driveway, the car lights and the light produced by the flashes of lightening showed us the crisis we were facing. The word "tornado" took on a new meaning for me when I saw our farm buildings in shambles. The machine shed that my daddy had built in 1945 was destroyed, along with an electric wind charger, a windmill, and a small storage shed. We were grateful when we realized we still had our home and beds to sleep in, even though the house had been moved six inches off its foundation. I didn't get too much sleep that night, because I was worried about my cats and dog. I'm sure your great grandpa was thinking about cattle instead of cats, how he was going to rebuild the shed and the chicken house, and what we were going to do for electricity.

The next morning brought sunshine and an end to the storm. Since we had no electricity, the electric fence was not working, so the first task was to find the cattle.

"Did you find them?" asked Brady, looking concerned.

"Yes, my daddy found them all standing in the far corner of the pasture.

"What about your cats and dog?" asked Earl Ray.

"I found my three cats hiding under a large piece of tin from the machine shed, and Lucky, our dog, lived up to his name: he survived by going into the barn where your great grandma and grandpa had once lived. The barn had not been damaged.

"What about the chickens since the chicken house was gone?" asked Josh.

"We rounded up the frightened chickens and put them inside a temporary mesh fence," I replied.

The after-effects of the tornado brought a new chore for me, as I had to walk around the yard and the pasture picking up nails, boards, tin, and other debris that the storm had scattered around. For a while, it was fun using a kerosene lantern to do my homework, but it was even better when we got electricity from an electric company.

Talk about character-building! I learned that, whatever happens, it is possible to bounce back with God's help, but it took many months of hard work to repair the damage.

One of the biggest disappointments from the tornado was the loss of the wheat crop. I remember going out into the field where the wheat should have been and hearing my daddy thank the Lord that, even though the wheat was gone, we still had a home to live in. He also thanked God for the provision that he knew He would give since we wouldn't have wheat to harvest and sell. The black thread of crises took on meaning as it blended with the other colors woven into the tapestry of my life, and I saw how my parents depended on the Lord.

It was challenging when it was time to plant a milo crop. Because of all the nails in the field from the tornado, your great grandpa had more than one flat tire on the tractor. It took stamina on his part to fix the tire and start planting again, just to experience another flat tire. When the milo was finally planted, he came back to the house, and we prayed for a bountiful harvest. God answered our prayer and gave an abundant milo harvest, which provided money for expenses, rebuilding the machine shed in 1948, replacing the windmill, repairing the house, taking care of other damage from the tornado, and buying groceries. Recovering from the destruction was difficult, but the Lord was my parents' strength, and He sustained them during this difficult time.

It will always be etched in my memory that no one who came for a visit or just dropped by for a visit left the farm without your great grandpa's praying with him or her. In fact, my daddy turned the hayloft where he and my mother lived before they built their first house into what he called his "upper room." Like Daniel in the Bible, he prayed three times a day in this special place of prayer.

The memory made me pause, and I looked out the window. "Hey, guys," I said, "look at the snow outside. It looks like we might be snowed in for days!"

"That's great, Grandma," said Earl Ray. "We can celebrate Christmas for more than one day!"

"Yay!" Luke cheered. "I hope we have that many gifts to open. Tell us about a fun Christmas that you had."

The Christmas I remember the most was when I was in the fourth grade and received a handmade Haynes Flute from my mother and daddy. Music came alive and took on a new meaning for me as I took lessons from a fantastic instructor, Nannette Pitman, a high school student in

Minneola. For three years she guided me along the path of fine arts and gave me a tremendous foundation of musical performance. When she graduated from high school, the search was on to find another competent instructor, and Nannette gave my parents the name of a professional instructor in Wichita, Kansas. I boarded the Greyhound bus to Wichita one Saturday a month at 5:00 a.m., took a lesson, and then came home. I remember my instructor saying, "Make your notes sing as you interrupt your music." I was only in seventh grade, and I went all by myself.

Music was a big part of our lives. A television was not a part of our home, so for entertainment and relaxation my daddy played his electric guitar while I accompanied him on the piano or played a duet with my flute. If anyone stopped by to say hello, we asked him or her in to enjoy the music we were playing. If they joined in, the musicale turned into an instrumental and vocal choir.

When I was in the seventh grade, I was asked to play a flute solo for a large teacher's reception in the Minneola high school auditorium. It was before the school had air conditioning and it was hot outside, so the windows were open to let in some air, although there were no screens on the windows. I do not recall the song I was playing, but after a six-measure rest, I took a deep breath and you will never guess what happened.

"What?" everyone wanted to know.

"Do you know how fuzzy a miller feels? Well, when I took a deep breath, a miller flew into my mouth. All of that miller fuzz stayed in my mouth when I spit out the miller. Yuck!"

"Oh, no!" Trevor said. "Did you finish your song?"

"Believe it or not, I did! After I bowed to the audience, I dashed for the water fountain in the hall to rinse out my mouth. Talking about it even all these years later still makes me feel the gruesome feeling of that fuzz in my mouth."

"I'm glad that can't happen to me," said Luke. "I play percussion!"

"Oh, Luke, you're so funny!" I laughed.

When I was in high school, I enjoyed the challenge of taking solos to league, regional, and state contest, as well as playing solos in church and for various events. My goal was to get a 1 rating every year, which I achieved every year except for my senior year, which was extremely disappointing. I forgot a small portion of the solo, "Concertino," by Cecile Chaminade, and when I finished performing, the judge gave me a 2 and said I would have had a 1 but for my lapse of memory. Even though I did not achieve my goal, I had the consolation of knowing I had done my best.

"I have been so excited and interested in telling you my story that I forgot that it may be time for our special Christmas Eve celebration," I told the grandkids. We had an annual reception with barbequed meatballs, sandwiches, a cheese ball and crackers, rocky road fudge bars, decorated cookies, fudge that Orlando usually made, and strawberry sparkle punch.

"Let's go! I'm hungry," said Earl Ray. "In fact, I smell barbeque. It must be the meatballs!"

"Who made the fudge this year?" Josh asked. "I can hardly wait to taste it, but I'm sure it isn't as good as Grandpa's fudge."

"That's a surprise," I replied. "Let's go and enjoy the food with the rest of the family."

Tin machine shed destroyed by tornado

Chicken coop destroyed by tornado

Tornado destruction

CHAPTER 5

That Girl and *That* Guy

"I have an idea," I said, as I watched my grandsons take their final bite of dessert. "Do you think we could find a way to get out of helping your mothers with the dishes? You see, if we don't get on with our story, we might not get finished before bedtime."

"Your story is more important than dishes," said Earl Ray, as his cousins nodded their heads in agreement.

"I know," Josh spoke up, "maybe our dads will help with the dishes. Let's sneak back into the cozy parlor, and we will never be missed."

"I call the recliner!" Luke said, running into the parlor.

"I'll sit on the wingback chair," I said, following the bounding boys into the room.

The tapestry being woven by the Great Weaver, God Himself, was becoming more uniquely colorful. It was during the Christmas holiday of 1949 when a young man by the name of Orlando Jantz came to Dodge City to visit his sister. His sister and her husband went to the same church I attended with my mother and daddy. Orlando's mind was definitely not on the service when he whispered to his sister, "See that girl singing in the choir? I am going to marry her."

"Was he talking about you, Grandma?" asked Brady. "Did he know you?"

"No, Brady, he did not. I had never met him, and we had never spoken to each other. It was pretty bold for him to feel that way, don't you think?

We were introduced after the service, but my mind was elsewhere, so I did not stick around. Guys, you are smiling. Are you thinking I was unkind not to have paid attention to a new person in church?"

"Well ..." they all said in unison.

"You mean you didn't stay around to see if he would ask you for a date?" Trevor interjected.

"Oh, no, there was another guy I was anxious to see before I went home."

I thought that would be the end of our encounter, but it wasn't. Your great grandpa thought the Great Tapestry Weaver needed some help, so in the spring of 1952, on a Sunday morning, my daddy matter-of-factly said, "We're going to church in Scott City."

"Why?" I asked.

"There is to be a special dedication service in one of the churches in Scott City, the Pilgrim Holiness Church."

Being the obedient daughter, I didn't ask any more questions, but I thought this was *very* strange!

When we arrived at the church in Scott City, I found out that *that* young man, Orlando Jantz, attended the church we were going to attend, and his parents were the pastors. Now, the tables were turned, and it was your great grandpa who was bold.

"It seems to me he had one motive in mind," said Brady.

"I know why," Coby surmised. "It is because he wanted Orlando to date you!"

"You are right!" I said.

That was the beginning of a blossoming romance. Oh, I must tell you: "that guy" was extremely handsome—tall, muscular, with dark curly hair. Wow, it makes me blush even now to think of him. I know you boys are giggling, but maybe someday you will meet that special gal, and you will understand.

My daddy lived by the rule that "if you are on time, you are late." He believed in being early to anything he attended. Because my daddy had given Orlando permission to come see me on weekends, Orlando met us at the Church of the Nazarene in Dodge City on Sunday mornings. By the time we arrived at church, there was always a green 1949 Chevrolet sitting in the parking lot with "that guy" who was stealing my heart in it. My daddy was impressed, as Orlando also believed in being early!

By then I could hardly wait for the weekends to arrive. During the week, as I went daily to the pasture to turn the windmill on or off, instead of pretending I was a queen sitting on a throne giving orders to all of her attendants, I was dreaming of *that guy*. Eventually, I tried to go to the windmill close to the time the mail was to be delivered so I could immediately go to the mailbox.

There wasn't a letter every day, but quite often, and don't ask me what he wrote in those letters, as it would make me blush! After graduating from Scott City High School in 1954, Orlando was to go to Colorado Springs Bible College in Colorado the next year. On our last date before he left for Colorado in September of 1955, we sat together, and I will never forget the song that was playing on the radio: "Three coins in the fountain,/ In the ripples how they shine./ One wish will be granted./ One heart will wear a valentine. Make it mine, make it mine, make it mine."

I wondered how my heart could wear a valentine when that special guy was leaving, but he promised he would be back. "Three Coins in the Fountain" became our song. I found it on a record (those were the days when one would play a record on a player instead of on an iTouch or iPod), and I listened to it every day and dreamed of "my heart wearing a valentine!"

In the spring of 1955, when I was a senior in high school, we took a trip before graduation. Guess where we went. Of all places, we went to Colorado Springs! The senior class sponsor gave me permission to meet Orlando and spend a few hours with him, and you can imagine that I was looking forward to those hours with anticipation. When he met me at the designated place, my heart fell because with him was his brother, who was attending the same college. I found out later that the college required every date to be chaperoned. After about an hour, Orlando gave his brother some money and told him that he wasn't needed as a chaperone any longer.

While Orlando was a freshman at Colorado Springs Bible College, he worked at a men's clothing store to pay for his college expenses. There were many months that he was the employee of the month for having the most sales. It seemed he had a way of convincing customers that they definitely needed shirts and ties to go with the suits they were purchasing. He was also good at convincing the ladies that their husbands needed new shirts for Christmas or advising her that Christmas wouldn't be complete without giving "her guy" a certain brand of expensive cologne.

During the time your Grandpa was in Colorado Springs Bible College, he was voted the most popular guy in the school! It was a tribute to his character and personality.

May of 1955 found me wearing a cap and gown; hearing my name, Naomi Ruth Kornelsen; walking across the stage; and receiving that long-awaited high school diploma from Minneola High School. Now I was intelligent, or so I thought. When I started attending classes at Bethany Penial College in Bethany, Oklahoma (later changed to Southern Nazarene University), I found out that I was not quite as intelligent as I thought.

Because Orlando did not want another guy stepping in and taking his place, when he heard I was going to Bethany Peniel College, he announced that he was going to transfer to the same college. When the President of Colorado Springs Bible College found out that he was going to transfer, he confronted Orlando with, "You mean to tell me that you are going to leave here after you were voted the most popular student in the college?"

Orlando's response was "Definitely, for, you see, the girl I am going to marry is going to be there."

Josh spoke up. "He went after what he wanted, didn't he? Were you thrilled he was going to attend the college you were going to attend?"

"'Thrilled' wasn't the word for it. You see, when Orlando held my hand, my heart beat like a big brass band!

"Hey, Ma," Coby said, "I know what that sounds like. The brass instruments in our band are extremely loud. In fact, I know what it feels like."

"What does it feel like, Coby?" I asked.

"They are so loud, I feel like the floor shakes under my feet."

"Oh, no, it doesn't," Luke said. "Her heart couldn't beat that loud."

"Yes, it did, Luke!" I said. "At least that's how I remember it."

Dating during our college days was difficult because Orlando held down a full-time job to pay for his college expenses. His parents were not able to contribute any money for his tuition, books, or room and board. His work and study load was very heavy, which didn't leave much time for dating. I remember going to the homecoming basketball game by myself. I felt sorry for myself, but it was exciting to wear the beautiful mum corsage he had given me, and I preferred going alone to going with anyone else.

During the summer of 1956, something exciting happened. Orlando and I were listening to our song, and he asked me to marry him so my heart could "wear a valentine."

"Did he give you a ring?" asked Josh.

"No, but guess what he did give," I said, knowing the answer would amaze them. "A set of silverware!"

"Silverware?" Josh said, his eyebrows raised so they disappeared under his dark brown hair, "I've never heard of that before."

"Maybe he wanted to be sure he wouldn't have to eat with his fingers after you were married," Coby said, giggling.

During the first semester of Orlando's sophomore year, he was on his way to one of his classes when he felt the Lord speak to him. The Lord said, "I want you to preach for me throughout the rest of your life. I will provide, and I will supply your needs."

When he told me, my first thought was that I did not want to marry a preacher and that Orlando was an odd choice for a preacher. "You, a preacher?" I said, astonished. "You are so shy that you hardly say anything when you are in a group." I should have known, though, that preaching would be his calling in life because he was majoring in religion. I also should have known he would be obedient to the Lord and follow His call and plan for his life. I decided that, if I wanted to marry him, I would have to accept being a preacher's wife.

We announced our engagement at the Valentine Banquet in 1957. Since our speech professor, Mrs. Baxter, had become special to both of us, she wrote the announcement and read it to the students and professors at the banquet. She then presented us, the newly engaged couple, Orlando Jantz and Naomi Kornelsen.

"Enough of the mushy stuff," Brady said. "What was your major in college?"

"I majored in business and had two minors, music and speech. I took piano, organ, and flute lessons."

"It sounds like you were definitely busy," Brady continued.

You'd better believe it!" I said. "Because I had not taken sufficient algebra in high school to meet college requirements, I had to take a make-up algebra class every Saturday of the first semester of my freshman year. The only time my schedule made it possible for me to enroll in the class was at 7:00 am.

"That was early!" Coby said.

"Too early. It was no fun to go to class when everyone else was sleeping."

With excitement, Josh spoke up. "I don't mind the mushy stuff. Grandma, don't keep us in suspense. When did you get married?"

"Before I get to that, I must tell you how hard your Grandpa worked so that he could attend college."

Orlando worked as a volunteer fireman in Bethany, Oklahoma. When he was on duty, he lived in an upstairs room of the fire department. When a fire call came, he and the other firemen slid down the fire pole, jumped on the truck, and with the sirens blaring arrived at the location of the fire.

During Christmas break of 1956 and the semester break between 1956 and 1957, he stayed in Bethany to make money for his junior year delivering mail on foot in the residential district. When I heard from him by letter or phone, he would tell me that he had to soak his feet every evening because of the blisters he got from walking his route. During your grandpa's junior year, he worked at the police department as dispatcher. As reports of crimes came over the radio, his job was to pass the information to various policemen and give directions about where to go.

Luke was in awe. "It sounds like 'Pa had a very exciting job!"

"Yes, your grandpa enjoyed it tremendously," I responded. "It was difficult keeping up with his college work, but he was allowed to study for his classes as best he could while he was on the job."

CHAPTER 6

From Wedding to Judge

The tapestry became even more beautiful when two separate cloths were stitched together on August 2, 1957, when that handsome guy, Orlando, and I were married in the First Church of the Nazarene in Dodge City, Kansas. After a short honeymoon in Branson, Missouri, we went to Southern Nazarene University to finish our education.

Your Grandpa was still working as police dispatcher to pay for his college education. Whenever the judge of Bethany, Oklahoma, was gone, Orlando was appointed as temporary judge. There were two policemen, twins, who thought the "college student judge" needed extra income. Because the judge got five dollars for every person who got a ticket, the twin policemen were diligent in watching for citizens breaking the law. During the time Orlando was the appointed judge, he was grateful for the extra tickets the twins issued—but I don't know about the townspeople who got them!

After we were married, I needed to help bring in money, so I applied for a job as the secretary to the judge in Bethany, Oklahoma. What a thrill it was when I was hired! Therefore, when your Grandpa was the appointed judge, I was his secretary. I will never forget when the message came over the police radio to be on the lookout for a certain make and color of car, and there was the possibility it would be coming through Bethany. Out the door dashed the twin policemen because they did not want to miss the opportunity to catch a murderer and his wife, who might have a body in the trunk of the car. It didn't take long for them to walk into the police station with a man and woman. One of the policemen ordered me to go in to the next room and frisk the woman to see if she had a gun.

Scared? You better believe it. I had never done anything like that before, but I didn't dare say no; that policeman was *big and burly*. The policeman promised me he would be right outside the door of the room where he was taking the woman, but that was of little comfort if she had a gun on her. I didn't know how to frisk, I did what I thought was frisking. I didn't find a gun or anything else unusual, but because there was blood in the trunk of the car, although no body, the couple were charged with first-degree murder. I never found out whether they were found guilty because it took a long time before the case went to trial.

In any case, I certainly didn't think frisking was in my job description. Maybe that was why I soon applied for a job as secretary to one of the county attorneys in Oklahoma City. When I was hired, I felt like I was climbing the ladder to stardom as secretary to a county attorney.

The opportunity came for your grandpa to work at the Oklahoma City Highway Patrol Department as dispatcher, and he worked there until he graduated from Southern Nazarene University. The patrol personnel tried to talk him into going to Highway Patrol School to become a patrolman, but since your grandpa was determined to be obedient to God, he declined.

So your grandpa was not only a preacher, he was a student, a mailman, a fireman, a judge, and highway patrol dispatcher. When he was younger, he worked for a farmer (when he was six), bringing the cows from the pasture when it was time for them to be milked. When he was ten and living in Lamont, Kansas, he worked for a farmer, driving a team of horses that pulled a hay wagon to take the hay to the shed to be unloaded. At twelve, in Lyndon, Kansas, he delivered the newspaper, *The Kansas City Star*. He had a three-foot-by-three-foot basket on the front of his bicycle where he put the papers, and when he had delivered all that his bicycle basket could hold, he went back to his home and picked up more papers. He delivered more than a hundred papers every day for two years. Since his mother and daddy didn't have the finances to buy him new clothes, he contracted to mow thirty-six lawns a week. His pay was two dollars for each lawn.

Your grandpa's mower broke down one day when he needed to mow, so his dad handed him the toolbox and told him to fix it. That's how he became a mechanic. Working at the corner grocery store was next on the list. At fifteen, he sacked groceries, worked behind the meat counter cutting pieces of meat that the customers wanted, and on Saturdays he went to work early and took orders over the phone from elderly customers who couldn't get to the grocery store. He filled their lists, put their names on the sacks of groceries, and delivered them in a Model T Ford truck that had to be shifted using foot pedals. All of the widow ladies wanted Orlando to deliver their groceries because he was so caring.

A few years later, he drove a tractor and planted corn. When he was a sophomore in Scott City, Kansas, his job again was in a grocery store, where he sacked groceries, stocked shelves, and then was promoted to checker. Many ladies wanted to come through his checkout lane because of his speed in checking and his congenial manner. During the summers of his junior and senior years, he worked for a land moving company driving a pay loader and scraping dirt to make the land level for irrigation. Besides the pay loader, he drove a caterpillar, called a push cat, to move the pay loader. In Scott City, he also joined the crew that would be building a large grain elevator.

"I didn't know Grandpa was qualified in so many areas," Josh said.

"It certainly made him skilled in many fields," Brady added. "I think his many jobs prepared him for what was to come later in his life."

Going over to the window and looking out, Luke said, "Hey, guys, there is enough snow that we could take a break and build a snowman."

"Yes!" they all hollered. "Let's do! And maybe even have a snowball fight!"

"I think we need a break," I said, "so dress warm, and we'll see how creative you guys can be."

Orlando & Naomi (Kornelsen) Jantz

CHAPTER 7

A Congregation of Cattle

After creating a unique snowman and being adventurous with snowballs, Luke came running inside, plopped breathless and exhausted on the floor, and exclaimed, "I've lost all my energy."

Grabbing a rocky road fudge bar, Josh, Brady, Trevor, Earl Ray, and Coby joined him and asked for more of the story.

August 3, 1959, brought bright, exciting threads into the tapestry that was being woven in our lives. Our first child, Deanna Sue, was born in Oklahoma City. With her dark, curly hair, she looked just like her daddy. I have to admit I was hoping she would look a little more like me, but her daddy was very proud. Since he had wanted a boy, I was happy he had the joy of having a daughter who looked like him.

We were in the height of our joy when, at six months old, Deanna Sue developed red dots all over her body. As parents, we were concerned. We were advised by a physician that leukemia was a possibility. You can imagine how our feelings spiraled downward. The tests that were run revealed that her blood platelet count was low, so she would bruise easily, but we were encouraged that it wasn't as bad as we had feared. The doctors suggested nothing be done at the time, but a yearly checkup would be a necessity. We loved watching her learn to walk and talk and admiring all her antics.

In May 1961 Orlando contacted Dr. Ray Hance, superintendent of the Kansas District Church of the Nazarene, to apply for a position as pastor. Dr. Hance told him there was a church that would have to be closed unless someone accepted the position as pastor. The person who accepted the pastorate would need to work hard to increase attendance.

"Would you be willing to take it?" Dr. Hance asked.

"Sure!" your grandpa told him. It sounded to me that there was a lot of work in store for us. Were we up for the challenge? Absolutely, but only with the help of God.

After loading our meager belongings into a U-Haul trailer, we moved to Ulysses, Kansas, in May of 1961, where Orlando would be the pastor of a Nazarene church with approximately twenty-five people attending. Even though there were not very many in attendance, we were excited to begin our pastoral position on June 1. Since the salary was $25 a week, your grandpa had to drive a school bus for extra income and work for farmers, and I gave piano lessons.

When Denise Marie came to join our family on October 26, 1961, the attendance of the church had grown to twenty-six. Because I was needed to play the piano, Deanna sat on the front pew, and our "sweet bundle from Heaven," Denise, slept in the bassinet at the front of the church.

Our church began to grow—first to thirty, then forty—and kept climbing.

Earl Ray interrupted, "I know why; it was because Grandpa was a great preacher."

"He should have been, Earl Ray," I said, "because every week he went into a pasture outside of town and practiced his sermons."

Being inquisitive, Coby asked, "Do you think he had cattle for his congregation when he practiced?"

"I'm sure there were."

"I imagine the cattle would respond with 'a moo, moo here, and a moo, moo there,'" laughed Trevor.

Congregation of Cattle

37

Our home was an apartment connected to the church. Since it only had one bedroom, Deanna and Denise slept in bunk beds at the foot of our bed, which provided "one way" traffic in and out of the bedroom. That one-bedroom apartment was challenging, to say the least, with two little ones!

During the winter months, it was normal for a glass of water or milk sitting on the windowsill to freeze, which made for a unique "frosted drink" during the night. Our home took on a heavenly look when we found snow on the inside of the window in the morning. Oh, the delights of our first parsonage!

As Deanna and Denise got older, they both sat on the front pew when I was playing the piano, which was interesting when I had to do some "parenting," as I had to leave the piano while the congregation kept singing. Since Denise was the mischievous one, it was she who got them into trouble! One day I needed to be gone for a short while to run an errand. Since your Grandpa's office was only a few steps away, I left Denise and Deanna in charge of dusting and vacuuming. To make dusting the furniture more intriguing, I hid pennies, dimes, and quarters under items on the furniture. They were so excited about finding these "treasures" that they started quarreling over who would dust and who would sweep. To this day, I don't know who ended up doing which chore, but I learned after the girls were grown that my bright idea almost resulted in a fistfight.

When I gave piano lessons in the family room, Deanna and Denise were required to sit quietly and play with their toys. I wanted them to be where I could keep an eye on them and know they were not getting into any trouble. I am grateful my piano students were patient.

Being young and a first-time pastor's wife carried with it interesting experiences. I thought the logical place to keep the brush I used to clean the commode was in the bathroom. However, when a guest speaker who was visiting our church and staying overnight with us came out of the bathroom after taking a bath and told me, "Your back brush is the best I have ever used," I decided that that brush should be stored elsewhere. I tucked that experience away in my mind as hilarious, as well as "what the guest speaker doesn't know won't hurt him."

Pastor Orlando had the ability to minister to many age groups. Teens loved him, so he was involved with teen camps during the summers. During the summer of 1964, while he worked at a camp for teens, I took Deanna to the doctor in Dodge City, Kansas, for a physical. The doctor's evaluation was that her blood platelet count was radically low and that she had to be admitted to the hospital. Blood platelets were flown from Wichita, Kansas, to be injected into her veins. The doctors advised that her spleen be removed in the hope that it would take care of her problem. We were not assured she would survive the surgery, but we committed and relinquished her future to our heavenly Physician. She made it through the surgery, and we were so grateful. The experience taught us a valuable lesson in the Sovereignty of God.

Part of your grandpa's pastoral responsibilities was to visit his members. Once, when Sam Dryer, a farmer, was having physical difficulties, your grandpa felt he needed to pray with him, but Sam had told him that, if he ever came to visit, he should not get out of the car unless Sam was available to keep his dog from being aggressive. When your pa drove into the yard, Sam was outside, which made Pa feel safe, but no sooner had Pa stepped out of the car than the dog bit him twice on the leg.

Calmly, Sam said, "Back up slowly and get into the car, and you will be okay."

Pa thought, "Now I've been initiated into my first visitation responsibility. He stayed, visited, and prayed with Sam. Then he went to the doctor, who treated the dog bites.

It was tremendously rewarding when the attendance of our church increased to ninety-eight after four years of ministry. Dr. Hance, the district superintendent, was thrilled and knew he had placed the perfect pastor in that specific church. Even though I thought he was perfect, it was only through God's help and a lot of hard work that the church grew as it did. It was a rewarding four years, so it was difficult to leave when Orlando received a call to be pastor of the Pleasant Hill Church of the Nazarene in Sylvia, Kansas.

We prayed and sought the direction of our heavenly Father, and in July 1965, we packed our belongings into a farm truck and moved to Sylvia. Tears were rolling down my cheeks as we drove out of town because I was leaving friends to whom I had ministered during the years we were in Ulysses. It was a tremendous consolation to know that marvelous progress had been made in the church during the time your grandpa was the pastor of the Ulysses church. As we left our first charge, we knew that the new couple who replaced us would continue to help the church grow.

CHAPTER 8

City Life to Farm Life

It was with some trepidation that we moved into our farm home in July. From city life to farm life? From an apartment to a big house? What were we going to do with all of the space? It did not take long to find out that the added space was thrilling. Deanna and Denise thought it was an exciting adventure because they now had more room to play outside. They became quite the tomboys as they climbed trees and pretended they were cowboys, chasing bandits down the-tree lined lane.

An interesting episode was in store for your grandpa during the first Sunday service in the Pleasant Hill Church of The Nazarene. Since we knew a couple who was attending the church, he asked the wife, Connie Moore, to pray the benediction. When the time came and she did not begin to pray, Orlando heard commotion in the sanctuary and he realized Connie had fainted. She recovered quickly and was just fine, but it certainly was not the way we had expected to begin the ministry of our second pastorate!

A special speaker was scheduled for a series of services not long after we arrived. I received word from the visitor, Rev. Willingham, that he needed a firm mattress on which to sleep. He would be staying in our extra bedroom, and the mattress on the bed wasn't firm but was thin and soft. Your grandpa went to the lumberyard and bought a sheet of plywood to put underneath the mattress, hoping it would meet the Rev. Willingham's requirements. After his first night, I asked Mr. Willingham whether he had experienced a restful night.

"That is the hardest bed I have ever slept on," He replied. Oh, my, what a way for a pastor's wife to make an impression! The next night we removed the plywood, and Rev. Willingham said that the bed was perfect. I tucked that experience, along with many others, away in the mental memories how to improve my role as a pastor's wife. He seemed to enjoy the meals I provided for him, which I hoped made up for his first night of pain.

Again, your grandpa had to supplement our income by working for farmers. When he was served a harvest meal of fried chicken, mashed potatoes and gravy, and several side dishes, all topped off with coconut cream pie, he felt it was worth the effort.

As I had done in Ulysses, I gave piano lessons. As I look back on all of the lessons I have given, I know that I have helped to prepare pianists to accompany congregational singing in churches, schools, and wherever needed. That is a rewarding feeling. I know the students' lives have been enriched, as many of them have used their music for their own enjoyment.

One year, after we moved in, the church congregation voted to build a new church in town. Your grandpa and other men in the church began demolishing the old country church, planning to use some of the lumber to build the new church, but suddenly they were swarmed and bitten by honeybees.

"Was there a beehive?" asked Trevor.

"Yes, quite a large one, but there was enough honey to be worth the risk of trying to sneak some for biscuits."

"Were you the one to get some of the honey?" questioned Earl Ray.

"No, I was definitely not going to risk getting bitten, Earl Ray. Your grandpa wanted some biscuits with honey, so he was the one who got the honey. We enjoyed biscuits and honey butter for several weeks. Soon the bees had to find a new home, since their present one was destroyed."

"I wish I could have some. I love honey-butter!"

"I know you do, Luke," I responded.

In 1967 the church was completed, and we found ourselves worshiping in a brand new sanctuary. Your grandpa and the other men in the church then had the exciting experience of building a home not far from the church for their pastor and his family and for future pastor families. I had the privilege of picking out the colors for the décor of our new home. The parsonage, known as the minister's home, would have a separate room for a guest minister or speaker who might be there for a series of services. And the bedroom would have a new bed with a comfortable mattress. I would not have to worry anymore about a speaker coming to stay in our home and sleeping on an uncomfortable bed. In 1969 we moved into our beautiful new home.

The church thrived under your grandpa's ministry. My daddy and mother enjoyed coming to visit and attending our Sunday services. Your great grandpa would say, "Orlando is the best preacher in the country! If there was a nationally known minister preaching in a city close by, I would rather go and hear my son-in-law preach." I was very proud, even if my daddy was probably a little prejudiced in that statement.

Orlando and I developed into an effective team as we ministered in the church. I held Bible studies with the ladies, led prayer groups, taught a Sunday School class, played the organ or piano or flute solos, made home visits with my pastor husband, and did whatever needed to be done. I even found myself entertaining in our home often, especially when a new family was visiting the church. To be sure the family felt loved and wanted, I had them over for a meal.

Orlando was a spectacular dad, as well as a tremendous pastor. He felt we should have not two children but many mouths to feed. You see, he loved his two daughters very much, but he also loved the other children in his congregation. He kept candy in his suit coat pocket so that, when children came to shake his hand after church, they received a treat.

Because I was unable to have any more children, we began the process of adopting a baby. I never felt very comfortable with this possibility, as I wanted another child of our own. As I prayed and sought the direction of the Lord, He gave me a scripture from the Old Testament. Abraham was feeling bad that he and Sarah didn't have any children, and God gave him a promise:

> *I will make of you a great nation* (Genesis 12:2).
> *Look now toward the heavens and count the stars—if you are able to number them. Then He said to him, so shall your descendants be* (Genesis 15:5).

> *Is anything too hard or too wonderful for the Lord? At the appointed time, when the season comes around, I will return to you and Sarah shall have borne a son* (Genesis 18:14).

I shared these scriptures with your grandpa and told him, "I feel God is going to give us a child of our own. I don't think we should adopt a baby." When our doctor's nurse called and told us a baby was available to adopt, we declined. I felt certain that, before too much time elapsed, we would be expecting another beautiful thread to be added to the tapestry God was weaving for our family.

One year went by, two years, and on and on. Finally, after about six years, I told Orlando, "I am sorry. Maybe I was wrong, but Sarah had the child God promised when Abraham was a hundred years old and Sarah was ninety. I want you to know, though, I *do not* want to be ninety when we have another child!" I also told him that I would keep believing God's promise. This experience gave me a great example to testify to the ladies' Bible study group: it is important to depend on and trust God to keep His promises and to believe He delights in giving us the desires of our heart.

Our ministry in the Pleasant Hill Church of the Nazarene was effective, and many people joined the church. Your grandpa officiated at several weddings and funerals and preached powerful sermons. It seems, though, there comes a time for all good things to end, and again it came time to pack our possessions and say goodbye to a wonderful congregation. New Year's Day 1971 found us driving west to Greeley, Colorado, to pastor another Nazarene church. It was hard because I got so very involved in the lives of the people where we were pastoring and we put down deep roots.

With our vehicle pointed west toward Colorado, tears once again ran down my cheeks, but just as with our last move, I was looking forward to meeting another group of ladies to whom I could minister.

CHAPTER 9

Marble Table To Wig

We were welcomed with warmth and love as we moved into our home in what seemed to us the very large city of Greeley, Colorado. Greeley was large enough to have a shopping mall, which was exciting, and it was also home to the University of Northern Colorado. As we had come from the rural farming community of Sylvia, Kansas, I felt Greeley was going to require a big adjustment, but the congregation of the Nazarene church made us feel immediately at home. We found our pantry filled with canned goods, staples, and candy for Deanna and Denise, and there was fresh fruit in the refrigerator. I felt as though I would not have to go to the grocery store for a month! Food never tasted as good as it did the day we arrived, when we were greeted with a delicious home-cooked meal.

Soon we became acquainted with our new church family and realized we were going to have a marvelous ministry. Since there was a college in Greeley, your grandpa had the exciting opportunity of ministering to college students, which was an extremely rewarding experience.

Because our church in Greeley was a larger congregation than the one in Sylvia, Orlando worked with a staff member—a pastor to youth and college students—which relieved him of some responsibilities that he would otherwise have carried.

There were many young couples in the congregation, which we appreciated. One of the tasks that your grandpa enjoyed as a minister was that of conducting weddings. He loved the romance and the excitement of the wedding ceremony and always wanted everything to be perfect. I remember once when, on the night of wedding rehearsal, the groom told him that he was going to be thirty minutes late to the wedding. Orlando said, "Oh, Brad, I know you are joking." Brad responded that he was serious, but your grandpa didn't believe him.

I was the organist for the wedding, and when it was time for the wedding to begin, your grandpa told me to keep playing the prelude. I played for five, then ten, then fifteen minutes and wondered how much longer I would need to keep playing the prelude. I could tell the wedding guests were becoming restless and wondering what was delaying the wedding. Then I thought, *Oh no, surely the groom wasn't serious. Will the bride leave? I don't have enough music to play for thirty minutes.*

Nobody left, but I'm sure the bride was becoming anxious. Exactly thirty minutes had passed when I heard commotion in the back and realized they were ready to begin the processional. What a relief! After that, the wedding went smoothly.

By this time, your grandpa was beginning to lose some of his curly black hair. He would always say, "I believe getting bald is like turning my head into a shiny marble table that is worth a thousand dollars!" Even though I may have been prejudiced in his favor, I believed him. Lance, the barber who attended our church, decided to take the balding of his pastor into his own hands and told Orlando that he had a surprise waiting for him at the barbershop.

"Don't keep us in suspense," excitedly spoke Earl Ray. "What was the surprise?"

Take a guess.

"I know," said Coby, "a wig!"

You're right!

The next time your grandpa entered the Marvelous Creations Barber Shop, waiting for him was a "marvelous creation" indeed, and Orlando walked out of the barbershop looking ten years younger.

"How hilarious," laughed Trevor.

By now Josh, Brady, and Luke were joining the others in howling laughter.

Well, the next day was Sunday, and because he did not want to hurt Lance's feelings, he wore the wig to church. I must say, he did look handsome. When the service started, he heard whispers throughout the congregation, and it wasn't long before the children and teens started giggling. Using the opportunity during the announcements, Orlando said, "I think I would feel more like myself, and hopefully Lance's feelings won't be too badly damaged, if I do this." Then off came the wig! The congregation clapped and cheered, and he never wore the wig again. That was a memorable Sunday morning service.

God has a way of weaving an extraordinarily beautiful tapestry, sometimes when you least expect it. I found out in January 1974 that we were expecting a baby! God's timing is an interesting adventure. Our new addition would be thirteen years younger than Denise and fifteen years younger than Deanna. We were all excited, and we waited with anticipation for the date to arrive.

Paige, a woman who attended our church, had a son with red hair, and she kept telling me that our baby would definitely have red hair like Nathan's and would have his temperament. I knew her "red hair" prediction would not come true because we did not have any red hair in our family, and I hoped our "bundle from Heaven" would not be as mischievous as Nathan.

On Sunday evening, October 6, I felt that it wouldn't be long before our long-awaited baby arrived. I passed this news on to your grandpa, who responded, "We are having communion this evening, and I need you on the organ, so please let our 'darling bundle' know he or she can't come until after the service." I played the organ, and then we went straight from church to the hospital.

Charlene Kaye came to join our family on October 7. It was 6:00 a.m. when your grandpa took Deanna and Denise to Winchels' Donuts and then off to the hospital to see their red-headed sister before they went to school. Paige was almost right, though I think her hair was more auburn than red.

Members of our church in Greeley and members from our previous church in Sylvia, Kansas, expressed their excitement for us with many cards of congratulations. Because one family in Sylvia knew that Orlando had been hoping for a boy, a card came addressed to "Charlie" Kaye Jantz, and ever since then, her nickname has been "Charlie." The minute "Charlie" wrapped her finger around her daddy's finger and he looked into her sweet eyes, he was thrilled because now he had a trio of girls. He knew he would not trade any of them for a boy!

CHAPTER 10

"Parson" and "Little Preacher"

In 1975, we found ourselves considering a move to Pueblo, Colorado. As we drove to Pueblo First Church of the Nazarene for an interview with the church board, I remember being impressed with the sign "Pueblo, next 13 exits." Remember, I was raised on a farm in a small community, and thirteen exits to a city seemed to be an enormous number to me. It was with the definite leadership of the Lord that your grandpa accepted the pastorate to Pueblo First Church of the Nazarene. We were graciously welcomed to our new assignment on June 1, 1975, and it didn't take long to become deeply involved in the lives of the people in our congregation.

As a pastor's wife, I never felt my responsibility was to sit on the sidelines. As our ministries grew, I became more and more aware that my role was to be my pastor husband's teammate. I started a Bible study for the ladies not long after we arrived, and because your grandpa felt prayer was a vital part of the growth of any church, I also organized an early-morning prayer time for anyone who wanted to attend. Soon the attendance increased from two to four, then six and sometimes more. Many felt the need to pray for the progress of the church. Prayer proved to be the key to many services anointed by the Holy Spirit.

Our Sunday noon meal became a time for entertaining new families. This also added to our success in increasing our church's attendance. My Sunday noon meals were not always without obstacles. One Sunday I was going to be entertaining a guest speaker, and I had also invited one of the families from the church. My main entre was Hawaiian chicken. When it was almost time for all of the guests to arrive, I was taking the Hawaiian chicken out of the oven, and it slipped out of my hands and dropped onto the floor. What a disaster! What was I going to do?

I had just washed the floor on Saturday, so I decided to scoop it up carefully and put it on my beautiful china meat platter. Everyone said it tasted scrumptious! I knew I would never do that again, even though I do not think anyone got sick, for which I was grateful.

Because I felt my appearance was important to the new ministry, I wanted to find someone who would do an admirable job with my hair and to whom I could also minister. How was I going to find such a person? To the yellow pages of the phone book I went. The Shear Haven Beauty Salon sounded interesting. With apprehension, yet confidence in God's leadership, I called and made an appointment. When I arrived at The Shear Haven Salon on February 14, 1980, I was introduced to Tammy, whose beautiful black hair and sparkling eyes and even more appealing, warm, inviting personality were stunning. When she had finished with my hair, I evaluated the hairstyle and knew I had found the person for whom I had prayed.

When I was paying for Tammy's services, she whispered, "I am moving to another location. Would you like to follow me?"

My immediate response was, "Absolutely!"

That was the beginning of years of friendship. My desire to minister was also fulfilled, as I spent time being a spiritual mentor to Tammy through weekly meetings for discipleship. Following the conclusion of our two-year weekly discipleship, Tammy expressed her thoughts about our time together: "It was an enlightening time of learning who God really is and discovering how to have a personal relationship with Jesus. I learned He loved me unconditionally and that He would help me forgive those who had hurt me. He healed my emotions, and I learned how to love myself for who I am. He forgave my past and helped me face the future with the knowledge that He would 'work out His plans for my life—for His faithfulness would endure forever' [based on Psalm 138:8]. I will forever be grateful for the lady who looked in the Yellow Pages of the phone book for a beautician."

During the summer of 1976, Orlando felt the need to hire a staff member for the betterment of the church's youth program and contacted

Rev. Mike Allen, a youth pastor in Casper, Wyoming. When Pastor Mike met Orlando in the Casper airport, Pastor Mike said the first impression he had of his prospective senior pastor came from a hearty handshake from large and comforting hands, a huge smile, and a warm, friendly hug.

Our heavenly Tapestry Weaver is very creative, and He weaves beautiful patterns. That was the beginning of five years of working together with Pastor Mike, praying for God's Kingdom, building the youth program of the Pueblo First Church of the Nazarene, and a lifetime friendship.

Your grandpa felt it was important to encourage the members of the church and to visit the homes of prospective new families. He thought a motorcycle would conserve gas, so he purchased a Honda motorcycle. Because Pastor Mike wanted to follow the leadership of his senior pastor, he bought one as well. Then, so they could keep in touch with one another, your grandpa and Pastor Mike each purchased a CB radio. Their CB handles were "Parson" and "Little Preacher." Mike's wife Judy once asked him, "If Pastor buys an airplane, what are you going to do?"

"Buy an airplane!" Mike responded.

"Parson" and "Little Preacher" used their motorcycles to build the attendance of the church by getting new, young couples to attend church. They took trips to the Rocky Mountains once a month, which proved to be a dynamic ministry. Part of your Grandpa's and Pastor Mike's goal when they decided what to do was to consider whether what they were about to do would get them any closer to their goal. I know they felt the motorcycle ministry was getting them closer to their goal of building God's Kingdom.

As a hobby, the senior pastor and youth pastor of First Church had an ongoing race to see who could pick up the most "road tools," that is, lost tools they could find on the side of the road. They collected screwdrivers, wrenches, and whatever other tools they could find.

"Who won?" asked Earl Ray.

"I think they thought each one of them had won the contest."

"Probably many of the tools out in the shed are some of the ones our grandpa found," added Trevor.

"I've heard about the candy dish that Pa had for the kids," Coby said.

"You're right," I replied. "If you had been around at that time, you would have been able to go into Pa's office after church and get some candy."

"Wow, that would have been fun."

"That is true," I said, "but there were probably parents who wondered why their children were not very hungry for Sunday lunch.

"Or, why they developed cavities," laughed Coby.

"Yeah," I laughed, "too much candy from the pastor's office!"

A marriage retreat and prayer retreat were two of the activities that built the solid foundation of the church. Your grandpa also wanted a discipleship program for the men of the church. What better way to minister, not only to the men but also to the community, than a drama?

I had heard of a drama titled "The Living Last Supper," so I began a two-year search for just the right one. I finally contacted one of my professors at Southern Nazarene University, Dr. Ruth Vaughn, who had written one that was fantastic; I knew it would be a tremendous ministry. My next challenge was how to get the men to participate. Through much prayer and "sweet talk," I got fifteen men and two ladies involved in presenting this powerful drama, and for three years we presented "The Living Last Supper."

This drama proved to be an effective discipleship for the cast as well as ministry to the community of Pueblo. The drama, a dramatic portrayal of the last day of Christ's life, takes place in the Upper Room, home of Micah ben Lazarus in Jerusalem, near twilight on the day of the Feast of the Passover, 33 A.D. In the drama, Micah ben Lazarus' sister has prepared the Passover Meal for Jesus and His disciples, but as the disciples make their way to the Upper Room, Micah ben Lazarus is adamant that he does not want them in his home. When Micah ben Lazarus meets the disciples, he realizes they are "changed" men, which enlightens him, and he also has a change of heart and mind. The Disciples are heartbroken to see Jesus take on the role of a servant by washing their feet, but when the Master serves them communion, they begin to realize the seriousness of the situation. As Jesus and his Disciples leave the Upper Room for the Mount of Olives, the Disciples are aware that they are on a mission they do not understand. In the Garden of Gethsemane, the audience is drawn into the torture Jesus knows He will experience in the hours to come, and the disciples are in agony when they realize Judas has betrayed their Master and is crucified. After the resurrection, as Christ appears to Mary Magdalene and Thomas, the audience is drawn into the thrill and excitement of hearing *"He is alive."*

"It sounds to me that that was a fantastic way to make Easter very enriching," Josh said after a pause.

"That is the purpose of discipleship, Josh," I replied. It is training for the followers of Christ. By using a drama, the cast turns their training into a ministry.

"Oh, I understand," interjected Brady. "When the cast presents the drama, they are making Easter more enriching for the audience."

"Yep, it is like taking an exam in school," Josh responded. "As a student, I hope my instructor is impressed with what I have learned, so the cast is using what they have learned and turning it into a discipleship for others."

I definitely have smart grandsons!

For several years, during the summers, I went home to the farm to help my daddy with the wheat harvest by driving the wheat truck. It was during these times that your great grandpa talked to me about moving back to the farm. He felt he no longer had the stamina to accomplish the work that needed to be done. I always lent a listening ear, but I never gave him any encouragement. Pa and I were happy doing what we felt was the most important work in life, that of being pastors."

I looked up at the clock and realized the hour had grown late. "Hey, you guys, do you know what?" I said, standing up. "It's midnight and time for me to get some sleep."

"We can't go to bed now," said Luke. "I want to hear the rest of the story."

"Don't worry, Luke; since we are snowed in and can't go anywhere, there will be plenty of time tomorrow. It looks like we have lots of beautiful snow out there. With the stars shining and the moonbeams glowing on the snow, it looks like there are millions of diamonds glistening on the snow. So good night! Sweet dreams!"

CHAPTER 11

Christmas Day

The sun shone on the snow-covered trees in the morning as our Kansas farm was transformed into a winter wonderland. We put on boots, heavy coats, and gloves and took a walk in the shelter belt of stately evergreen trees. There was no wind, and it seemed each tree branch was whispering, "Look at me and see the beauty God has created." When we went inside, we found a breakfast of cinnamon rolls and orange juice waiting for us to eat before we opened presents.

Luke, being the youngest, opened his present first. "Look what I can build!" he shouted. "An airplane with LEGOs! I also got a black pocket knife!"

Coby was next. "I got a cordless drill!" he said, jumping up and down. "This is awesome!"

What did you get, Earl Ray?" asked Brady.

"I got the pheasant that I shot, stuffed and standing on a log from the farm."

"Trevor, it is your turn," I said.

Trevor ripped open his package and cried, "Wow! I got a coin bank Grandpa made. Now I can save my pennies and nickels! He used to make lots of them and give them as gifts."

"What did you get, Brady?" I asked with a smile.

"Look! A socket set!" Brady said excitedly. "Someday, when I have a car of my own, I can put the set in the trunk and have a wrench handy to change a tire or work on my car when I need to!"

"Earl Ray, you aren't the only one who received a stuffed pheasant," said Josh after opening his gift.

"Did you shoot it?" asked Coby.

"Sure did!" Josh answered.

"As a reminder, guys, we cannot forget what Christmas means," I said. "It isn't just exchanging gifts."

"I know," Luke boldly said. "It is celebrating the birth of Jesus!"

"Luke, you are correct. I am proud of you."

After the excitement of opening presents, we enjoyed our Christmas dinner of turkey, dressing, mashed potatoes and gravy, sweet potatoes, pretzel salad, green beans, and pecan or blueberry pie for desert.

"Are we too full for more of our story?" I asked.

"Oh, no!" the boys spoke in unison.

It was August 1985, and my daddy, the Rock of Gibraltar in my life, was diagnosed with cancer. As he lay in the hospital in Dodge City, he looked me straight in the eye and asked, "Are you ready to take over in time of crisis?" I knew what he meant. He was asking whether I was ready to move to the farm.

Your great-grandpa lived for only two weeks following the diagnosis. One of your dads told the story of my daddy well: "a very humble beginning—farm machinery, cattle, hay, a young married couple, the sounds and smells in the hay loft where they lived." My daddy's words in the hospital were from John 3:30: "He must increase, and I must decrease." That was his way of life. He lived not for himself but to bring honor to his heavenly Father.

Now the prophetic words of my mother that "someday you will be living here on the farm" came back to me. *Decision time is here*, I thought. After my mother moved from the farm to town, we had locked up the buildings and made arrangements for a wonderful friend to take care of the farming, but as Orlando and I went back to our church family in Pueblo, we began praying for God's leadership for our future.

On February 6, 1986, your grandpa was struggling with the fact that, if we moved to the farm, he would be leaving his beloved church to another pastor. He would also have to give up his position on the Nampa Nazarene University College Board of Regents, and the District Advisory

Board of the Colorado District Church of the Nazarene would need to appoint another district secretary, a position he held at the time. When he met with one of the general superintendents of the Nazarene church for advice, Orlando said, "If this is God's will, I will follow His leadership."

The general superintendent, who was very supportive, assured him that God would be faithful and give guidance. Your grandpa also struggled with the fact that he had never farmed a day in his life, and farming was not a lucrative way to provide for a wife and children. Another thought that seemed to make the idea of moving difficult was that the district Colorado record showed that Pueblo First Church of the Nazarene was having record average attendance of 293 in the morning worship service. Your grandpa wondered, "Do I want to leave my wonderful church?"

For the next eight months, Orlando and I prayed and journaled, seeking the answer for our future. We found it in the Bible:

> *So do not fear, for I am with you; do not be dismayed, for I am your God. I will strengthen you and help you; I will uphold you with my righteous right hand* (Isaiah 41:10). *Do not set your heart on what you will eat or drink; do not worry about it* (Luke 12:29). [We heard: "Go forward unafraid!"]

> *I can do everything through him who gives me strength* (Philippians 4:11). [We heard: "The way will open as you go. No circumstances can harm you in any way. Do not let fear assail or depress you. Useful work lies ahead of you."]

> *The Lord will guide you always; he will satisfy your needs in a sun-scorched land and will strengthen your frame. You will be like a well-watered garden, like a spring whose waters never fail* (Isaiah 58:9). [We heard: "Face each difficulty, however great and seemingly unconquerable, as you go forward toward it. Know that all is well."]

But it was scary, as we knew there would be no weekly check, and we would have some emotional and painful months. Then the Lord seemed to speak to us from Matthew 28:18: *"Go and make disciples of all nations,"* and we heard, "I will give you more and more people to speak to about Me," so the, the decision was made: We *must* move to the farm. Even though the future was uncertain, peace calmed our minds, and we knew the decision was correct. Eleven memorable years at Pueblo First Church of the Nazarene came to a close.

We did not have the money for a moving van, so we moved using the 1971 Chevrolet wheat truck, which took four trips, nine hours each way. On July 2, 1986, we were a sight for inquisitive eyes as we pulled off Highway 283 to the dirt road leading to our future residence, pickup loaded, and the wheat truck/moving van piled high with our belongings.

We moved from a beautiful, spacious home in Pueblo to a small, two-bedroom, one-bathroom farm home on the flatlands of Kansas. No welcoming committee greeted us, no hot meal or bouquet of flowers awaited us, no groceries were in the refrigerator to make us feel welcome, but we knew we were greeted by the King of Kings and Lord of Lords. What more could I ask? He had promised to provide for us, and we knew He would. We would live by faith.

The first several months included many difficult days of adjustment, as finances were limited. Many times, I sat in my car in the grocery store parking lot and prayed, "Dear Jesus, I know I don't have enough money to buy what is on my list, but give me wisdom to get what You know I need." I would come home knowing I didn't get everything I wanted but that I had what was necessary.

I learned to put meals together for people who stopped by for a visit and was reminded God could do the impossible. He used "bony pieces of chicken" that produced meat that multiplied like the loaves and fishes in the Bible.

Your grandpa was kept busy working for a neighbor and being a supply pastor on weekends. He also drove the school bus for the Minneola School District. The-part time job was a necessity and one he would keep for the next twenty-two years. The students who rode the bus thought he was a fun bus driver and called him O. J. When there was a special trip, they asked for O. J. to drive their bus. They loved him, and he felt the same way about each of them who were under his care.

The large activity bus was his favorite bus to drive, as he enjoyed taking teams to football, basketball, and baseball games and the band to the state fair and other events. There were even times I was able to ride with Pa in the activity bus.

"I remember that bus," hollered Luke. "Pa took me for a ride several times."

"I heard Grandpa talk about the teams wanting him to be their bus driver to games."

"I know the teams thought he was one of the best, Brady," I said.

"He took me for a ride too," interjected Coby.

Wistfully, Earl Ray spoke up, saying, "I wish I had lived close enough for him to take me for a ride."

I was grateful I could be close by to take care of my mother. She had chosen to move to an apartment in Dodge City, and it was wonderful to help her with whatever she needed.

The first big task on the farm's agenda was to plant wheat in September. It was July 10, 1986, when your grandpa realized the generator was not working on the Case 830 tractor and would have to be fixed before he could plant wheat. By seeking wisdom from his heavenly Father and talking to a tractor repair shop employee, he was able to get the tractor in working condition.

When your grandpa went to plant wheat, his request for me was to "pray that the wheat seed planted will produce a bountiful harvest." I carried out his request. The rest was in the hands of our Great Provider and the Master Weaver of our lives.

In the fall it was time to harvest the milo crop, for which we needed a combine. Finding one that we could afford would take much prayer and wisdom. After searching high and low, your grandpa found a Gleaner Baldwin that he knew would be suitable. It had been used by another farmer, but it seemed to be in useable condition, and it was.

At 6:00 p.m. on November 20, 1986, your grandpa finished cutting his first milo harvest. We knelt on the ground by the combine and thanked the Lord for what we felt was a bountiful harvest. It made 59.7 bushels per acre, and we were grateful and excited, expecting a large amount of income. However, we were discouraged when our check was much less than what we felt we needed. I was reminded of Matthew 6:25–29: "*Do not worry about your life, what you shall eat or drink or wear. Look at the birds of the air; they do not sow or reap, and yet your heavenly Father feeds them. And why do you worry about clothes? See how the lilies of the field grow. They do not labor or spin. Yet I tell you that not even Solomon in all his splendor was dressed like one of these. Your heavenly Father knows just what you need."*

After having our first Thanksgiving at the farm with our family, we realized our home was far from adequate in size. Even though we had much for which to be thankful, it was hilarious when Orlando and I and our children, your parents, tried to become presentable for the day. For once, I was grateful my daddy had built a "two-seater" outdoor bathroom, although no one wanted to use it. The tiny bathroom, with its miniature tub, small lavatory, and peeling wall paint, simply wasn't adequate to the task. The next week, we began contacting individuals concerning remodeling the miniature cramped quarters in which we were living, but a friend from Dodge City pointed out that remodeling would not be wise. The house was so old that it wouldn't be worth the money it would cost to remodel.

January 7, 1987, was a momentous day. The foundation was dug for a new home! The contractor was a friend who helped with the framing of our new home. Your grandpa was going to install the sheet rock, but a friend of a friend from Alaska came our way and relieved him of that big project. A professional electrician from Pueblo saved us a lot of money by not charging us for his labor, and another friend put in the heating and cooling system. Each friend helped to weave another part of God's plan.

On March 2, 1987, our house began taking on the look of a beautiful home when a man from Cheyenne, Wyoming, came our way and laid the brick for a minimal price. A neighbor husband and wife team also helped in many ways.

"What about the church-pew woodwork," asked Earl Ray, referring to the baseboards, window framing, and wood trim.

"Yes, your grandpa made it all out of old church pews. He did a superb job!"

"Where did he get the church pews?" asked Josh.

"Whenever a church wanted to give away or sell their pews, your grandpa tried to get them, as he knew they would provide some fantastic lumber.

"Wow, that sounds like a lot of work to me."

"It was, Trevor. He had to take the old wood stain off the pews and plane them so they were ready to use. Then he re-stained the wood with an oak stain and used his woodworking tools to make all of the decorative woodwork and trim.

"I have heard you say this is the house the Lord built," Coby said.

"That is definitely how I feel, Coby. We could never have done it on our own."

But even as we were excited about the progress of our new home, we were reminded that life doesn't always seem fair. It was Sunday, July 19, 1987, at 8:18 a.m., when my darling Mother went to be with her heavenly Father. She had been my mentor, and her departure left a huge void in my life. I've tried to fill that void by doing my best to brighten the corner in which I live as much she did hers. The fragrance of her Maker permeated any room she entered, and my hope was for that to be true of my life as well.

As much as I mourned her passing, the year passed quickly with all the work we had to do as we prepared to move into the home in which you are now listening to your grandpa's and my story. On November 24, 1987, it was finally moving day, from a home our heavenly Weaver provided to a home He helped us build. It was truly a dream come true!

CHAPTER 12

Diversified

To being a farmer, a bus driver, and a supply pastor your grandpa added the challenging role of being a youth pastor for the teens in Minneola, Kansas. Needless to say, our lives were becoming enriched in many ways. We had marvelous helpers who helped provide the type of music teenagers could relate to, and those two years that we served gave us an experience that helped us stay young. Your grandpa was definitely diversified.

It seems to me that pastoring churches was his vision. From March to September 1992, he was the interim pastor of the Stafford Calvary Baptist Church. It was a rewarding ministry that members of the congregation, your grandpa, and I thoroughly enjoyed. Your grandpa and I were also fulfilled in spending four years conducting a discipleship Bible study with the husband and wife team who helped us when we were building this home. It was a tremendously fruitful experience in our lives, as well as theirs.

Then, as if we weren't busy enough, we felt called to a new ministry to the community, a ministry that included another chance to bring the "Living Last Supper" drama to life. The ministry was wonderfully described in the April 6, 1988, newsletter of the Dodge City Church of the Nazarene by Rev. Stan Meek:

> Check in your dictionary for superlative words to help me describe our "Living Last Supper," written by Dr. Ruth Vaughn, presented Friday and Saturday nights—expressions such as majestic, tremendous, dynamic,

impressive and above all, <u>sacred</u>. Approximately 600 attended. Many marveled that our church had many men who could perform so ably. All of us who had a part give God the glory. Naomi Jantz was the director, inspiring, caring, and carrying an exhausting schedule, that we might receive a dynamic blessing from the ministry.

The "Living Last Supper" was effective for seven years, for six of which the drama was presented in the Little Theatre of Dodge City Community College. I feel honored to have been able to touch so many lives through this avenue. It was fulfilling for me, as I felt it was a discipleship for every member of the cast. I also enjoyed being able to share the events of the last day of Christ's life with a huge audience.

The threads that are used in the weaving of a piece of tapestry are not always colorful; some are dark and drab, and others are like the colors of a rainbow. One night we heard raindrops, and we thought, "Oh, how wonderful!" But then we heard something hard hit the roof. Hail! How sad we were when we went to look at our wheat crop the next morning. It was gone! Your grandpa and I stood out in the field, tears running down our faces, but we felt in our spirit that our needs would be provided for. Since God had promised to provide for us, we were reminded that the situation was God's problem, as well as ours. The next morning, I wrote in my journal:

> The sun is shining after the storm as I sit outside with my Friend, Jesus. He is the One directing the "well trained Bird Symphony and Choir." They are performing just for me. So many varied voices, and the Master Conductor has taught them to blend and harmonize as they sing. They obey and follow their Conductor by never missing a cue. What marvelous calm and peace I feel, knowing that my Friend has creative ways to provide for us. Matthew 6:26 says, *"Look at the birds of the air; they do not sow or reap or store away in barns, and yet your heavenly Father feeds them. Are you not much more valuable than they?"*

We saw our needs being provided for through the kindness and generosity of our neighbors, who gave us meat, groceries, and even cash. Wow! God's resources are more than adequate. Even one of your grandpa's part-time jobs brought a miraculous answer to a serious problem. The property taxes on the farm were due, and your grandpa took a check to the office in Dodge City, where he was to pay the taxes, but it was three hundred dollars short. However, when he came home from his part-time job in the afternoon, he showed me a check for three hundred dollars that his employer had given him, saying, "We've never done this before and probably will never do it again. Here is a bonus for you." Miraculous and unimaginable joy was ours.

Regardless of what else was happening in the world, we knew the Lord would provide. He even sent me back to college, but this time as a teacher! On January 9, 1989, I began teaching elementary school music at a community college. It was a rewarding experience, even though I felt overwhelmed at times. I enjoyed being able to teach prospective elementary school teachers the important role the fine arts play in the lives of students.

I felt as diversified as your grandpa when I became an employee in the business office at the Minneola District Hospital after I was no longer employed at the community college. While I worked at the hospital, I made many friends I still enjoy today. After I was no longer able to work in the business office at the hospital, I was grateful when the number of my piano students increased to twenty, as I believe in the adage that says, "To teach music is to touch a life forever."

Even as we worked odd jobs to get by, we felt a calling that would stretch our finances and our faith. My daddy had been unable to purchase an eighty-acre parcel of land that joined the farm on the northeast, but a rainbow-colored thread was added to the tapestry of our lives when, on January 2, 1987, Orlando, your parents, and I knelt on that eighty acres that we had been privileged to purchase. We dedicated it to God and gave Him thanks for making this awesome experience possible. Even though your great-grandpa was not given the privilege of experiencing the answer to his prayer, we felt honored to participate in that answer. Depending upon the rotation of crops, either wheat or milo is planted on that portion of the farm to this day.

On September 20, 1990, another marvelous possibility presented itself to purchase the eighty acres that adjoined the farm to the northwest. Despite the opportunity, fear paralyzed our thoughts, as we wondered how we could pay for it. Isaiah 41:3 became very meaningful to us: "*I am the Lord who takes hold of your right hand and says, do not fear, I will help you!*" We realized that no one who is identified with Jesus Christ should suffer from doubt or fear, and it became evident to us that we must have absolute, perfect, irrepressible, and triumphant faith!

Through much prayer and the gift of a banker's having confidence in us, we were able to take out a ten-year loan to purchase the second eighty acres. However, even after the eighty acres were ours, we were fearful. How would we make payments? In the past, the crops had not been adequate, money was lost on the sale of cattle, and the bank account showed zero. What had we been thinking? For that matter, what had the banker been thinking?

> *Arise from the depression and prostration in which circumstances have kept you—rise to a new life! Shine (be radiant with the glory of the Lord). For your light has come, and the glory of the Lord has risen upon you.* (Isaiah 60:1AMP)

We relied on our faith in that scripture. We knew God had wisdom and that, no matter how challenging our circumstances were, He would provide. We were also aware that God is sovereign, and He is not wringing His hands wondering how He is going to take care of us—He *knows*—so worry is unnecessary.

Your grandpa also did farm work for one of our neighbor friends, and he had the privilege of being in charge of the Singles' Ministry at our church, for which he received a small salary. He sold cattle (this time for a miraculous profit), and God chose to kiss the crops with the beauty of His touch. Every time a payment was due, God provided, and each year, after we made the loan payment, we gave thanks to our heavenly Father for His provision.

It was a fulfillment of God's luminescent rainbow of promise when we were able to pay off the loan in eight years instead of ten. God had worked a miracle!

> *Obey me and do everything I command you, and you will be my people, and I will be your God. Then I will fulfill the oath I swore to your forefather, to give them a land flowing with milk and honey—the land you possess today.* (Jeremiah 11: 4–5)

On November 26, 1999, your grandpa and all of our family stood on the northwest eighty acres, dedicated it to God, and burned the mortgage.

"I remember that," said Brady. "We rode out there on the hay wagon."

"Yep!" Luke said. "Pa read scripture, we sang a song, and then we stood in a circle holding hands and thanked Jesus for the land on which we were standing!"

"It was cold, but it was fun, wasn't it?" I said. It was exciting to realize my daddy's dream of having the farm together, for a complete section had now been accomplished.

CHAPTER 13

Outdoor Church

In October 1992, a member of the Session, the governing body of the Presbyterian church in Kingsdown, Kansas, asked your grandpa if he would preach for two Sundays. Then he was asked to be the interim supply pastor for three months, then six months, then a year, then for as long as he felt God would lead him to be the pastor.

Those years were very fulfilling. In fact, the members of that church as well as the Presbyterian church in Bucklin, Kansas, became an integral part of our lives, bringing enjoyment and fulfillment. There were many opportunities for us to minister, which often came in disguise. For example, I loved to entertain, and even that turned into a unique opportunity. During 1994, we observed single adults' birthdays and couples' anniversaries in our home on the last Sunday of each month. We had an annual picnic in our shed during the fall season, which provided a time to build intimate relationships. Games made our evening one of laughter and fun! Orlando always gave a devotional that led to spiritual growth.

We went to Bucklin at 9:45 a.m. on Sundays and Kingsdown at 11:00. He also spent time during the week encouraging and praying with people who were in the hospital and doing his best to contact those who were not attending church. He wanted to see the churches grow in attendance.

A spectacular event each year was the Walnut Grove Service, which was held the first Sunday of June. The service, held outside in a beautiful walnut grove, was always uplifting and rewarding. It reminded me of the Biblical account of Jesus preaching to the multitude on the mountainside, but instead of the five loaves and two fishes one of the disciples brought

Jesus to bless, your grandpa blessed a bountiful table of food that was brought by those in attendance. I do not think there were twelve baskets of food left over as there were in the Biblical account, but I know no one went away hungry from the picnic under the trees.

"Was it fun to have church outdoors?" It was very inspirational, Trevor. In fact even the songs of the birds blended harmoniously with the voices of individuals in attendance as they lifted their voices in song. "I wish I could have been there," wistfully spoke Earl Ray. You would have enjoyed the tranquil setting as you would hear the gentle sounds of the trickling brook. Your Grandpa's sermon was stimulating as he spoke underneath the majestic walnut trees.

CHAPTER 14

A Rainbow after the Storm

Even as we weathered the financial storms in our lives, we couldn't imagine the storms ahead. Still, we knew that, no matter the strength of the storm, it's only after the storm is over that we see the brilliant colors of a rainbow in the sky.

The same concept happens in our lives. We do not see the creative purpose that God has for us until a difficult circumstance in our lives has passed. It is at this time that we are able to realize that God has engineered the painful crises, the lessons it brings, and the relief that follows.

On November 20, 1996, I had a mass removed from my body, and a week later I was told that the mass was cancer. That dreaded word! I would need to have surgery. I was devastated; this was a severe storm!

I was reminded in my devotions as I read God's Word that Jesus would still the storm. I was also reminded that my name was written on the palm of His Hand. Would I be able to see the rainbow after this storm? No matter how harsh the storm, I knew God would keep me from sinking:

> *Those who hope in the Lord will renew their strength. They will soar on wings like eagles; they will run and not grow weary, they will walk and not be faint.* (Isaiah 40:31)

Two weeks later, on December 4, 1996, as I went into surgery for a mastectomy, the Angels of the Lord surrounded me, and I felt them holding me. Orlando's voice gave me comfort and contentment as he read to me, prayed for me, and told me how much he loved me:

I love you, God—you make me strong. God is bedrock under my feet, the castle in which I live, my rescuing knight. My God—the high crag where I run for dear life, hiding behind the boulders, safe in the granite hideout. I sing to God, the Praise-Lofty, and find myself safe and saved. (Psalm 18: 1–2 MSG)

I went into surgery knowing that someday I would see the beautiful colors of the rainbow that would add golden threads to the tapestry of my life.

That Christmas, my daughters were a fantastic help in cooking dinner! Even one of their husbands got in on it, helping to make the dinner rolls for our family meal.

During those painful days, the Lord reminded me: "*Now I rejoice in the midst of my sufferings*" (Colossians 1:24 AMP). It was revealed to me that trouble never comes to anyone unless it brings a nugget of gold in its hand. What would the nugget of gold be for me? I knew it would be the deepening of my character and that I would be given the privilege of "bearing fruit" for my Savior.

I know that others will learn from my painful experience as I share the four primary lessons I learned through this difficulty.

1. Oswald Chambers said in his book, *My Utmost for His Highest*, "God can never make me into wine if I object to the fingers He uses to crush me. God could only use His own fingers, but sometimes He chooses to use circumstances to which we would rather not submit. If we are ever going to be made into wine, we will have to be crushed; you cannot drink grapes. Grapes only become wine when they have been squeezed."
2. At the time God chooses, He will make all things beautiful by removing the emotional pain.
3. I realize everything that comes into my life can be used to influence others to live the victorious Christian life.
4. I must be hopeful even though the branches of my life are made bare by bitter adversity; I must look up into the unfathomable

depths of the Father's love. It is only as the leaves are stripped from a tree branch by the storm that I can see more of the blue sky.

Oh yes, I must tell you about the rainbow. Three weeks after surgery, I asked the surgeon when I could start practicing my flute again, as I was to play a flute duet with Charlene at Southern Nazarene University for her senior recital in March. The surgeon told me I could begin any time, as it would be tremendous therapy.

Therapy? I thought he must be joking. The doctor didn't tell me that therapy, even doing something I loved, could be so painful, and I learned that success comes with much pain and perseverance. With many tears, I practiced diligently so I would be able to accomplish a goal worth striving for. I was determined! Then, on March 4, 1997, at Southern Nazarene University in Bethany, Oklahoma, the rainbow appeared. How beautiful it was! The duet was fantastic. The privilege was afforded me to accompany Charlene on her final solo, "His Eye Is on the Sparrow."

You've heard about the special pot of gold at the end of a rainbow? If there is such a thing, mine came the evening of dress rehearsal for the recital. At the close of the rehearsal, Charlene's flute instructor, Feodora Steward, asked me to come to where she was sitting. *Oh no!* I thought. *What did I do wrong? I must not have played according to her expectation.* However, her comments to me were ones of affirmation, and then she asked me if I knew who she was. I thought for a moment, and I responded with astonishment when she said, "You took lessons from me when you were in college." It was not until the evening of dress rehearsal that I realized Charlene and I had taken flute lessons from the same professor!

My rainbow was doubly colorful, and it definitely had a pot of gold! The physical pain I had endured in preparation was forgotten, replaced with iridescent threads added to the tapestry of my life by the Great Master Weaver.

CHAPTER 15

Impossible made Possible

It seems I couldn't get "The Living Last Supper" drama out of my system. My vision was to involve several churches in the community in a single cast. Since I lived in the Minneola area and the cast had always been from the church we were pastoring, the idea of staging a wider-ranging drama seemed nearly impossible. Since I didn't know men in the area other than those in my own church, how would I decide who fit which part? How would men who were not acquainted with me respond to me? Maybe my most worrisome issue was whether the cast would have confidence in me as a director.

Again, I turned to the Scriptures: *"As I was with Moses, so I will be with you"* (Joshua 3:7) and *"My wisdom is all you need. My strength comes into its own in your weakness"* (2 Corinthians 12:9). The words could not have been clearer: I felt that I was being told that the Lord could fulfill my dream once again and that, after seeing the drama, the audience would say, "My life will never be the same; Easter has a brand new meaning for me."

I knew that no excuses could stand in my way and began interviewing people whose names had been given to me by various pastors. Several people I approached were more than reluctant to participate. They gave me answers like "I can't act," "I can't talk in front of people," and "I get stage fright." The most common response was "I've never done anything like that before."

I bit my tongue to keep from replying, "There's a first time for everything," and instead replied, "I'm just looking for ordinary, rugged individuals who are willing!"

After much prayer and wisdom from God, I chose the cast; fifteen men and one woman. We had our first night of ministry at the Christian Church in Bucklin, Kansas, with a packed sanctuary on April 9, 2004. The "Living Last Supper" was presented two evenings each year for three years. In 2007, the ministry was moved to the Bucklin High School auditorium, where it was presented for two more years.

The responses to the drama were awesome, tremendous, marvelous, and definitely spirit-anointed! Even Orlando accepted a role, portraying Micah ben Lazarus, the keeper of The Upper Room where Jesus and the Disciples met for the Passover Meal. The part that made me the most nervous was that of Judas Iscariot. Who would want to play that awful, important role? Thankfully, when I approached Don Dupree, he responded with "Whatever you need me to do." My feelings were that of relief and admiration for anyone who would undertake that daunting task. His portrayal was authentic. He felt he was sharing the costly message of what it meant to betray the One who gave His life to save humankind.

"If I am asked again," he later told me, "count me in!"

I replied, "Maybe you don't know it yet, but you are in for life!"

Even with such a terrific response from the church community, I wasn't sure what to expect when I was approached about bringing the "Living Last Supper" to the Civic Center of Dodge City. I felt like Bezealel, in Exodus 31, when he was asked to make artistic designs for the Arc of the Testimony and felt incapable of accomplishing the task. After seeing the huge Civic Center auditorium, I felt inadequate. The Spirit of God filled Bezealel with skill, ability, and knowledge. Those qualities would also need to be given to me.

The Drama was used as a powerful ministry to a large audience. The Lord had impressed me to ask Rob Scott to portray Christ. After much consideration and prayer he accepted. It was an awesome task to accept this role as it needed to be someone who would characterize the compassion Jesus felt for His disciples when He told them, "I must die; it is a part of God's plan." It was important for this individual to portray the agony Jesus experienced in the Garden of Gethsemane. He would need to draw the audience into the sensational moment of the excruciating pain Jesus would have experienced. Rob was dramatic in his portrayal of Christ.

Various people who attended the drama described their feelings: "I felt I was in the presence of Jesus"; "every time I see the 'Living Last Supper,' I gain a new insight into the Biblical account of the Easter story"; and "I realize the disciples were just ordinary, 'rag tag' men who were used by Jesus."

Because your grandpa was unable to participate in the drama in 2010, Josh Roesener, who was from Dodge City, portrayed Micah ben Lazarus. Josh's life was changed dramatically by his participation. He became radically dedicated to serving the Risen Savior, and in the years that followed, he never even considered missing the opportunity to participate whenever the drama was presented. The ministry of this dramatic production was becoming powerfully influential. God does not always work in common-sense ways so much as in supernatural ones. He delights in doing the impossible with people who are willing to be used in a unique way.

CHAPTER 16

Finding Gold

"Wow! Look outside," I said as I watched the winter sunlight sparkling crystal clear like it can only in western Kansas. "The sun is still shining, and it looks like it is getting warmer. Let's continue our story in the clubhouse your grandpa made for you in the shelter belt."

"I'm on my way!" hollered Coby.

"I'm driving the four-wheeler," chimed in Brady.

"And I call for riding on the back," Luke added.

Once inside our "forest clubhouse," I brought out the pads that I had taken along to make our stump seats a little more comfortable; being Grandma, I also made sure we had blankets and snacks. The boys clamored for more of the story.

Your grandpa always picked up stuff on the road or wherever he saw something he thought could be useful. The top of this clubhouse was the top of a pickup he found in a ditch. I wondered what he was going to do with his new treasure, but one day he told me he was going to build something for the grandkids. When it was finished, I saw he had used his "gold nugget find" for the top of the clubhouse.

One of the thoughts that God gave to us as we were praying about moving here was, "I will give you more and more people to speak of Me." That was becoming true in various ways. Your grandpa was ministering in the community, and he was asked to perform weddings for young adults who had become acquainted with him through his school bus driving for the Minneola School District. It was a thrill for him to participate in those exciting events.

He was also asked to conduct the funerals of people who had come to respect his "shepherding gift." One of his marvelous attributes was the ability to comfort families who were hurting. I have read that radical obedience has no lead in its heels. In other words, when God asks us to do a certain task, like for us move to the farm, we do it quickly.

Even as we worked hard to be obedient to our calling, your grandpa still had time to pursue a little bit of fun. He loved to go hunting and to work in his wood shop, and sometimes he made gifts. I think each of your mothers has a post office box bank that he made, a gift that I know they treasure. It seemed, though, that he never had as much time as he would have liked to work in his shop. It would have been his joy if he could have trained one or two of you to use his shop tools.

"I know," Coby said. "Even though he helped me build a bird house, I still wish I could have built a desk with his help."

"Yeah, me too," Brady added. "It would have been fun for him to help me build a cabinet for my room."

"You know the base he made for a night light out of walnut wood?" Luke said. "Then he put a telephone pole insulator in the oven, heated it up, and put it in cold water to make it look cracked and decorative. I wish he had taught me how to make one. I would have given it to my mother for a present."

"It would be fantastic if I could make your wishes come true," I responded. What I can do is tell you about your grandpa's wish that came true.

In June of 2004, your grandpa wished for a super wheat harvest. Two weeks before harvest, he checked the wheat, and it seemed to be shriveled. He checked it a week later, and it was the same. We all hoped and prayed that the wheat would produce better than we feared it would. When the harvest was finished, we knew a miracle had taken place, as the test weight of the wheat—that means the pounds per bushel—was 55.6.

That test weight, meant your grandpa would have more bushels to sell than we thought! Amazing! We thought of the promise in Psalm 94:22: *"The Lord honors those who obey Him."*

Of course, the wheat crop wasn't always fantastic. The next year the wheat was hailed out, and we didn't have any harvest at all. Still, we knew God would be our Provider! When trouble comes, faith clings to His character. As it says in 1 Corinthians 10:13: *"God is faithful."* Even though we were saddened by the loss of the wheat, we knew God was able to take every circumstance and use it for our long-range good. We knew He would not always work to make us happy but to fulfill His purpose. We also knew that, even though God delights in giving us joy, we needed to realize that "Jesus is enough"—in fact, *more* than enough. Those were difficult lessons of trust for us to learn.

Jesus would continue to be enough! In 2007, we were blessed mightily by the Lord when we had a record harvest. I brought a letter with me that your grandpa wrote to his three daughters, which describes the blessing it was to us, and our farm. I reached into my pocket for the letter, unfolded it, and read it aloud.

> *To My Dear Girls,*
>
> *I want to give you an update of our harvest, which will prove to you the powerful God we serve. One of our fields planted to wheat was 65 acres. It made 81.6 bushels per acre. After cutting the entire crop, it all averaged 76.5 bushels per acre. Now, remember, the insurance company gave me fourteen percent hail damage, so taking that into consideration, had it not hailed, it would have averaged 87.2 bushels per acre. Incredible! We've had our lean years and even a total hail out, but God rewards and makes up for it.*
>
> *When we came to the farm, we could hardly make it financially, but God gave me the promise and encouragement that, if I worked hard, He would provide. I started preaching at two churches, drove a school bus, and farmed the best I could to make a living. It was nearly a seven-day workweek*

(counting Sunday as church work). Now, God says, "I'm going to reward you with an incredible wheat crop." We give Him all the credit. We sowed the wheat; God watered and multiplied the seed. Unbelievable! God performs the impossible. This is the largest crop this farm has ever produced!

I know it was all the prayers that Naomi's father, Willie, prayed all through the years. He committed this land to the Lord. After each harvest, when we finish cutting, we pray in the field and thank God for His bounty and give Him the glory. Thank you to all my family for your many prayers for us and the farm. God rewards; praise His Holy Name!

Love,
Daddy

A few short weeks after the wheat harvest that year, Orlando and I were on our way to Alaska to celebrate our fiftieth wedding anniversary! How exhilarating it was to take off on the big jet from Wichita and fly above the clouds. I was reminded that I may not see the sun shining below the clouds, but the magnificent view above the clouds proves the sun is shining whether I see it or not.

I will never forget the experience of sailing on a huge cruise ship. I discovered that glaciers are not small icebergs but snow packed approximately a hundred feet thick. Some glaciers are a mile wide, and a portion of them may be six hundred feet below the water.

As impressive as the sights all around our ship were, the sights inside were almost as magnificent. It is hard to believe, but fifteen hundred sandwiches were made each day on the cruise, along with three hundred cakes and pies served each day and ninety gallons of ice cream. On August 2, when our server brought us one of those cakes to celebrate our anniversary, we could hardly believe that fifty years had gone by so quickly.

After fifty years together, the old saying that "trouble never comes to someone unless it brings a nugget of gold" continued to be true. I'm not talking about the kinds of "nuggets of gold" that your grandpa would bring home, like the old truck hood that serves as the top of this clubhouse. The nuggets I am talking about are those we found in our daily walk with the Lord. They were more than we could have imagined. Instead of treasures found or even money earned, we found strength beyond our perception, a gold thread added to the tapestry of our lives that I will share after we go back inside.

"My feet are cold," I said. "Even though the air is refreshing, and we have enjoyed our snacks, I vote for the indoors. How about you?"

"I call for driving the four-wheeler this time," said Earl Ray.

"The rest of us will race you back," hollered Josh.

CHAPTER 17

My Continuous Trust Is in My Heavenly Father

I settled myself in the rocker once again, with Josh in the wingback chair, Brady on the couch, and Earl Ray, Coby, and Luke on the floor.

On December 14, 2009, I wrote in my journal, "If my life is spiritually vigorous, I cannot believe my circumstances simply happen at random. I must see every situation as the means of obtaining a greater knowledge of Jesus Christ because He is sovereign.

Orlando had been diagnosed with esophagus cancer. A mass in the lower part of his esophagus had been found and would have to be removed. Was there to be a dark thread added to our life's tapestry?

We knew that, when we are without strength emotionally and physically, we can still be dynamite because of who our Master is! We also knew that He who knows the paths of a hundred million stars knows the way through the whirlwind and the storm in which we found ourselves. Jesus promises *never* to let go of our hands!

After consultation with three doctors, Orlando had surgery in January 2010 at the Kansas University Medical Center in Kansas City to remove his esophagus and make a new one from his stomach. It was a radical surgery, and your grandpa was concerned he wouldn't survive it. In fact, he even wrote a note to his girls and me with a final message.

We relied on the Word, and its promises, like Psalms 93:4, *"Mightier than the thunder of great waters, mightier than the great breakers of the sea— the Lord on high is mighty!"*

I was grateful when a friend made it financially possible for our three girls to be in Kansas City with your grandpa and me. Even through my tears, I saw the beautiful rainbow colors of God's love.

Orlando survived the surgery, but he would have a long road of recovery. During his recovery, we realized that it is through the painful times of life that we learn the greatest lessons. His progress seemed to be slow—learning how to eat, not being able to eat much, losing weight, and trying to gain strength. The day he came home, February 1, 2010, was a tremendous celebration! The farm had never looked as fantastic as it did on that monumental day.

What I used to think was normal had taken wing and flown away, and I learned a new normal. It was a privilege to take care of the love of my life. I knew the road ahead wouldn't be easy, as Orlando's physical body would take months to heal, and the emotional trauma even longer. Through the realization of God's sovereignty, I knew deep in my heart that the suffering would give way to a bright, new future. Two great gifts had been given to me: my valentine was alive, and God's love had sustained us. These would be days of Thanksgiving as I held his hand, read to him, and told him how much he was appreciated. I treasured the moments we spent reminiscing.

As a farmer, your grandpa had powerful hands. As a pastor, they were caring and compassionate. When he shook hands with those who had attended church on a Sunday, they felt a warm, firm grip that conveyed with one squeeze strength and integrity. As a carpenter, his hands were flexible and sure. In the roles of dad, grandpa, and husband, his hands were loving and tender.

Day by day, Orlando's strength began to return, and your grandpa was soon able to eat three small meals a day. Our claim became Psalm 92:12–14a (AMP): *"The righteous will flourish like the palm tree; (be stately, upright, useful, and fruitful); they shall grow like a cedar in Lebanon (majestic, stable, durable, and incorruptible). Planted in the house of the Lord, they shall flourish in the courts of our God. (Growing in grace) they shall still bring forth fruit in old age."*

We were given many opportunities to share with those who came to visit how God had directed us and woven His plan into the fabric of our lives. After three months, the day came when your grandpa was able to be back in the pulpit. He was weak but thankful. Even though his strength was limited, he conducted a funeral for one of the parishioners at Kingsdown and performed a wedding for a couple at our Bucklin church. He was very grateful!

We thought all was going well, but it wasn't going as well as we thought. He seemed to be gradually losing strength.

"I know Grandpa always enjoyed having cattle," recalled Earl Ray. "Did he have any again?"

"They were his pets, weren't they?" Josh asked.

"I remember Pa always called the cattle *busters,*" said Luke.

"And he took us with him many times on the four-wheeler to feed them," Coby added.

"All of you are correct. Even though he might not have had the strength to lift the fifty-pound sacks of feed for the cattle, Randall Spare, the veterinarian, had a herd of black heifers delivered for your grandpa's enjoyment."

Orlando—herd of black angus heifers

Even as he slowly returned to the life he'd once had, he began having difficulty swallowing and had to be put on a feeding tube. On Sunday, March 20, 2011, following our church services, both Bucklin and Kingsdown churches prayed for your grandpa. We stood in a circle of love during this time of prayer. We went to Kansas City the following Wednesday for a checkup, as your grandpa had been feeling very rough.

The report he gave to both churches on Sunday, March 27, was a difficult one to share:

> Naomi and I wish the report in Kansas City had turned out differently. I have no doubt that God is still sovereign and, thus, very much in control. Why the report of the oncologist turned out to be more difficult than I would have liked, I do not know, but my faith and trust in God is still as strong as ever. I was told that the cancer has returned and is very aggressive. Because it is not curable, chemotherapy is not recommended.
>
> The morning before we went to KU Medical Center, the scriptures that the Lord gave to me were Deuteronomy 31:6: "*Be strong and courageous. Do not be afraid or terrified because of the difficulty, for the Lord your God goes with you, He will never leave you nor forsake you*" and Psalm 46:1: "*God is my refuge and strength, an ever-present help in trouble. Therefore, I will not fear! Jesus said to me, 'Peace. Be still. Do not be afraid, though the earth give way and the mountains fall into the heart of the sea, you need not fear!'*"
>
> Praise God, I am His child, and I know however long the Lord allows me to live, He has promised to take care of me, and He is the Pilot of my life. I desire to assure my church family that my continual trust is in my heavenly Father. He provides and cares for me. My desire for you is to stay focused on your Savior and serve Him to the best of your ability.

The members of our churches showed their love and compassion for their pastor and me. They sent cards, stopped by for visits and prayer and brought food to us. We felt fortunate to have such compassion bestowed upon us after nineteen years of pastoring these two fabulous congregations.

The handsome young man I dreamed of when I walked in the pasture as a teenager had been the most wonderful husband I could ever have imagined.

Even though the oncologist had told me that I did not have long with my husband, I held on to the thought that maybe she was wrong, but in the stillness of the night on Wednesday, May 6, I walked around the yard with my dog, Cody, and told him, "I'm afraid soon it will be just you and me." God's voice then came to me, and the brilliant colors of God's rainbow of love hovered over me, bringing me comfort. Through the storm of my tears, I heard Jesus say, "I am your banner, and I am Jehovah Jireh, your Provider." I saw His protection covering me, and in the quietness of the night, I heard everlasting, heavenly music. Just as God appeared to Isaac in Genesis 26:24 in the night, God appeared and revealed Himself to me. I could not hear God's voice during the thunder of my grief, only in the quietness of my spirit. I realized I could not be so concerned with my personal cares that I forgot the faithfulness of the One in charge. I remembered also that I had daughters and grandchildren who needed me.

On Thursday, May 7, Orlando said, "Reach out and grasp all that God has for you, and never give up. You mean the world to me; I love you so much. Jesus will always be my Savior." A few days later, he said, "I don't know what the future holds or what God has in store for me, but I want you to know that whatever He wants is what I want. I have always loved you as my wife, and I always will."

Your grandpa would say to you, as he said to your mothers and me as we stood around his bed, "What's everybody sniffling for? Why are you crying?"

The words from Psalm 27:13 and 1 Peter 1:6–7 were a great comfort:

> *When you grow faint in the fierce fires of affliction, do not try to be strong; just be still and know that I am God. I will sustain you and bring you through.*

> *In this you greatly rejoice, though now for a little while you may have had to suffer grief in all kinds of trials. These have*

come so that your faith of greater worth than gold which perishes even though refined by fire may be proved genuine and may result in praise, glory, and honor.

On Sunday evening, May 22, a group of friends from the Minneola Community Church came to our home and sang hymns of testimony and encouragement. Orlando felt very privileged. He even preached a short sermon. (He could never pass up an opportunity!)

All three of or our daughters were here, along with you, Earl Ray, when on Tuesday, May 24, 2011, at 9:04 a.m., my companion of fifty-three years was relieved of his suffering. After fifty years of preaching, he went to be with his heavenly Master to live a new life. He was healed and free of pain!

"I miss him terribly," Brady said, tears running down his cheeks.

With a trembling voice, Trevor said, "When I put pennies and nickels in my bank, I will remember Grandpa and how much he enjoyed working in his shop."

"And I will remember Pa taking me on the four-wheeler to feed the cattle," Luke added.

Nothing felt right without the love of my life. It was as if the contentment and love I'd known for so long had died with him. I made it through the following hours, numb with grief. He had been my best friend, and he made me feel safe. I felt like Humpty Dumpty, fallen and broken so badly that I would never be put back together, and that the tapestry God had been weaving of our lives would no longer be beautiful.

I found that these words from the book *Calm My Anxious Heart* by Linda Dillow, helped ease my pain:

> *Leonardo da Vinci was an artist of great skill. When he was a pupil studying under his master painter, the master called Leonardo to him and asked him to finish a painting the master had begun. The man had grown old and felt the time had come to quit painting. Young da Vinci had such reverence for his master's skill that he was overwhelmed by the suggestion that he should add his strokes to the master's. The*

> *man said simply, "Do your best." Trembling with emotion,*
> *Leonardo seized the brush and knelt before the easel to pray.*
> *"It is for the sake of my beloved master that I implore skill*
> *and power for this undertaking." As he began to paint, his*
> *hand grew steady and his eye awoke with slumbering genius.*
> *He created a masterpiece.*

I now knew that I would be able to live, and with the help of my Master Weaver, my life's tapestry would become a masterpiece.

Getting up from the floor and giving me a hug, Coby said, "Ich liebe dich, Ma!"

"You remembered, Coby; I love you too!"

"We all love you!" Josh said.

"Thank you, Josh."

Many friends, family members, and acquaintances came to pay honor and respect to your grandpa at his funeral on May 27, 2011. The Minneola High School Gym, the largest space in town, was hardly big enough to hold everyone.

Terry Janson, general manager of the Victory Electric Cooperative, wrote a tribute for Orlando:

> From the first time I met Orlando Jantz, I knew he was
> a bright man, but soon realized he had a quality that far
> exceeded any personal characteristic a person could have.
> That characteristic was kindness and compassion. Orlando
> was one of the kindest, most compassionate people I ever
> knew. He became a friend about fifteen years ago out of
> necessity, because Victory needed someone to stand before
> our members and open our annual meeting with prayer.
> Out of that experience, a friendship was created between
> Orlando and me. The friendship grew and he became
> a valued friend of the cooperative; as well as a friend to
> many of our employees. Orlando's kindness and caring
> spirit just consumed people and made you want to be his

friend. I am so fortunate to have had the privilege of his friendship for these years. He honored the cooperative by giving the invocation for the annual meeting through these past years. He will be greatly missed.

Kansas District Superintendent Dr. Edmond Nash wrote:

> Orlando was a wonderful pastor who reflected the highest and best of his calling to be a shepherd to God's flock. His congregations did not lack for pastoral care. His love for people was evident as he effortlessly moved from situation to situation within his charge. Beyond that, he was a good and faithful minister of the Word. His people were fed the "bread of heaven" with love and without compromise.

Randall Spare, our veterinarian, gave a tribute to your grandpa at the memorial service:

> Orlando lived out his faith daily; he trusted God in an explicit manner. I know God found great pleasure in Orlando's faith. I would describe him as a shepherd, which was evident as he took care of the cattle that I put on his pasture. The last time I delivered cattle, his family helped him get into his motorized scooter. He made a beeline out to the fence to look at the calves. He wanted to make sure they would become accustomed to his voice as he called, "Here, busters." That same shepherding quality was even more obvious in the churches he pastored. I personally have experienced his tender care in the time of heartache as well as joy in the good times.

Dr. Tony Luna, Orlando's attending physician, shared:

> Orlando loved life, his family, his friends, his bus kids, and his Honda motorcycle. He loved his vocation. His mission in life was to bring the story of salvation to others, and to show God's love and compassion. In all aspects of

life, he mirrored the love and patience of God. It has been said the last great freedom in this world is the freedom to choose your attitude. Orlando's faith in God was the basis of his profound joy while walking in the "valley of the shadow of death." He faced death with the confidence of knowing that eternal life in Heaven was waiting after the passage from this earth.

Pastor Mike Allen, who was Orlando's associate pastor in Pueblo, came from Oregon to conduct the memorial service. He made the following statements:

Pastor was a Godly man—easy to love. He was an unusually wise and discerning man. I was nurtured and mentored by my senior pastor. He modeled well the concept that we must have cool heads and strong faith in the time of crisis. This carried me well in the years to come when I became a senior pastor. As I would look across my desk at my staff in a meeting, they did not see me, but they saw the image of my pastor friend from Pueblo. I knew in those staff meetings that I did not want to disappoint my Lord, nor did I want to disappoint my former senior pastor and friend. I will miss his advice. My last goodbye was said standing in the front yard of his beloved farm in Kansas, just a short time before he joined the Church Triumphant. My last tribute to him was leaving a wrench in the driveway of the farm. I just wanted him to know, "You won, Pastor! You found more tools that I found!" Yes, it is difficult to say goodbye, but I will meet him in Heaven one of these days.

After the funeral, my days were clouded with grief. I took walks around the farm and prayed. It was during one of those walks, with tears flowing down my cheeks, that I envisioned, like a whisper in my heart, ̇ ̇ ̇ ̇ ̇ through a beautiful meadow with my sweetheart, but it wasn't ̇eart; it was Someone else walking beside me. He took my hand in His and reassured me that He would be my *Ish*, the Hebrew word for husband, my heavenly Husband. He would take care of me and be my Provider. After that, my emotional pain was still severe, but my steps were a little lighter, and instead of being clothed in black, I realized I was wearing the iridescent colors of the rainbow.

I knew Jesus wanted to infuse His Presence into my thoughts and that challenging times were ahead that would be opportunities to trust my heavenly Husband for wisdom. There were days when it seemed fear had me in its grip. I knew the name, Naomi, meant joy, but would I ever experience joy again? When fear gripped me in its tentacles, I did my best to replace it with praise for my *Ish* and to turn my fear into joy.

As before, I was comforted by scripture:

> *The Lord, my powerful God, is with me. He is mighty to save. He will take great delight in me, He will quiet me with His love, He will rejoice over me with singing* (Zephaniah 3:17).

> *The Lord will work out His plans for my life, for His faithfulness endures forever* (Psalm 138:8).

Even in my grief, my prayer and desire were resolute:

> *Cause me to hear your loving kindness in the morning, for on You do I lean and in you do I trust. Cause me to know the way wherein I should walk, for I lift my inner self to You. Teach me to do your will, for you are my God; let your good (my words: kind, sweet, gentle, wise, comforting) Holy Spirit lead me.* (Psalm 143:8–10 AMP)

Since I knew my heavenly Husband would take care of me, I would do my best to step out into the future with Him. I knew that the people He would send to provide that care would surprise me.

And I was right.

CHAPTER 18

Surprises

In the weeks after the funeral, my emotions were broken and torn, but I found that the heavenly Weaver of my life was also the great Heart-Mender. The morning of June 14, 2011, I read somewhere that, "When God allows difficulties to come my way, He is not trying to make things hard; He is just trying to get me into a position to bless me." Wow! My question became, "So, what is going to happen today?"

It didn't take long for me to find out, as the pressure pump for my water went on the blink, and I didn't have any water. *Oh, no,* I thought, *what else could go wrong?* Then I noticed there was a lot of water on the north side of the grain tank (better known as the silo). A water pipe had burst. Would surprises bless me? How long would it take?

Then the dog barked, and a pickup drove into the yard! The first surprise person! I made a phone call, and three more surprises arrived! The men did their best to fix the problem, but had no luck. The problem seemed too big for us to solve.

That evening with no water, I used the outside privy. Your grandpa had turned the dreaded two-seater outside bathroom patriotic by painting it red, white, and blue and putting a flag inside with a sign that read, "Before you do anything else, stand up and salute." It also had a patriotic curtain for the window. Since it hadn't been used for a while, I knew that mice may have nested in there, but mice nests or not, the patriotic outside privy was the only answer.

I thought maybe devotions would give me encouragement, but the that was brought to my attention made me laugh:

For our light, momentary affliction (this slight distress of the passing hour) is ever more and more abundantly preparing and producing and achieving for us an everlasting weight of glory (beyond all measure, excessively surpassing all comparisons and all calculations, a vast and transcendent glory and blessedness never to cease!) The things that are visible are temporal (brief and fleeting). (2 Corinthians 4:17, 18a AMP)

I remember thinking, *Light affliction?* I was thankful my heavenly Husband had a sense of humor.

Three days later, with the water still out of order, I had another surprise visit when a school teacher from Minneola Grade School came to the house with a bucket filled with water and a mop to clean the "patriotic privy" so it would be more inviting. She definitely was an angel!

Thankfully, I did not need to use the privy forever. A water well and service man came to evaluate the problem and advised me that it would be costly to take care of the situation because it would require a different type of system than what had been used. I claimed the promise in Isaiah 41:13: *"Do not fear, I will help you."* My need was evident. God's provision was already in place, and my bad time would be His opportune moment!

My provision came as another pot of gold at the end of a rainbow. The water well serviceman said he would donate his time, and other "surprise individuals" would pay for the supplies. My needs were being supplied!

I wasn't given much time off before another difficulty arrived, and a wind, hail, and rain storm damaged the roof of my home. How rewarded I felt when the Community Church of Minneola provided the finances to cover the repair of the roof, as well as the roof of the chicken house that had been my parents' first home.

I was beginning to realize the dark threads in the weaving of life's tapestry are as needful in my Master Weaver's skillful hands as the gold, silver, and other bright colors to weave the pattern He has planned.

When the time came for our annual wheat harvest in June 2011, I wondered if there would be someone who would surprise me and help with this huge task? I received a phone call from a friend, who said, "You need to come see the unique development in your wheat field." What a sight:

three John Deere combines, three semi wheat trucks, and a grain cart all lined up in a row. It was a welcome sight and a healing balm for my spirit.

However, even as the farm's needs were being met, I realized that, while your grandpa had been a tremendous famer and preacher, he had also been my coach. He told me so many times, "You're doing great. The task you accomplished was superb," And I began to realize that Orlando lived his life like a coach, encouraging everyone he met. Nothing gave him more pleasure than rewarding even the smallest accomplishment with the words, "I'm proud of you!"

I needed to learn the lesson that sometimes God allows circumstances in our lives to redirect our path on the "gold-paved highway of trust." I learned a valuable lesson as I saw that trust can turn adversity into a colorful path He has planned.

"Hey guys," I said, "do you ever have any problems?"

"Absolutely!" responded Trevor, "I have trouble having time to do my homework."

"Yep, practicing my piano when I do not want to," Luke added.

"Do you think that, by then, I had had enough difficulties come into my life?" I asked.

"I think so!" answered Earl Ray.

"I thought so as well, Earl Ray, but on June 28, I became aware that a third of my home was sinking, and I asked myself whether this was also part of the beautiful path planned for me by the unique Weaver of my life's tapestry"

I discovered that God had a colorful path of friendship planned for me. An acquaintance by the name of Twiggy became a close friend, affirmer, and coach during the days when I needed someone to listen and when I needed guidance. It seemed she knew exactly what to say to give me encouragement: "You are strong! You can do it! I know there will be direction to take care of the situation, even if it seems impossible now. You are doing great! Life is a game! Go for the goal!" She became my coach.

With the help of family, friends, and experts in the field of foundation repair, I saw my enormous problem solved. The finances were provided beyond my expectations. Twiggy's response? "I am proud of you; the impossible situation became possible."

Then life began to get uniquely interesting! On July 8, I saw that the basement ceiling was wet and knew that water must be leaking from somewhere.

It became an opportunity to receive a gift of friendship. My friend Pansy, whom I met while working at the Minneola District Hospital, sent me a note that said, "Never give up! You are being held in the shelter of your Master's presence. Rely on His energy and guidance. He is throwing His arms around you, lavishing attention on you, and guarding you as the apple of His eye. He has written your name on the palm of His hand. Give your worries and cares to Him. He can be trusted." Pansy was a friend to be treasured.

Oh, yes, adversity turned into a "gold-paved highway of trust." A plumber found out that four loose screws in the tub faucet upstairs had created a big problem downstairs. Sometimes a small oversight can create a large difficulty if left unattended.

Then came August 2, 2011, our wedding anniversary. I knew on this day that soon I must close the door to the past with grace. Close the door with courage. It wasn't easy to face tomorrow when I felt so alone, so I must remember that I am not alone, because I am told, "*I am with you always*" (Matthew 28:20). I did not know whether I could close the door to the past with grace, but I was going to do my best.

If I was going to do my best, I had to celebrate our anniversary. Your grandpa and I often enjoyed going to the Dodge City Days Rodeo for our anniversary, so on August 3, 2012, I enjoyed the best rodeo in the state of Kansas.

I was in the stands enjoying the rodeo when a storm began to brew. I thought, *I need to go home*, so off I went to the farm. I was almost to the dirt road leading to the farm when a severe storm hit. The lightening showed me the entrance to the road to the farm, but I became stuck in the mud, so I rode out the storm on the dirt road. Being by myself even made it more frightening, so I was grateful that I had a cell phone to call for help and that a compassionate neighbor came in his four-wheel drive pickup, took me home, and went back to get my car.

Oswald Chambers said, "My circumstances are ordained by God. God in His providence brings you into circumstances that you cannot understand at all, but the Spirit of God understands. The difficult circumstance will be turned around for your long-range good."

Ordained? I wondered. *Long-range good?*

When I reached the farm, I found a mess. The buildings were damaged, and the shelterbelt looked terrible, as the hail had stripped the trees of their branches, and there was debris all over the yard.

Okay, God, I remember thinking, *you wanted "gold paved trust," so I'm going to try!*

Remember when God told me, "The people I send you will surprise you?" Well, that is exactly what happened. A few days later, I was on the phone with one of your mothers, sharing my heartache for the farm with her. She was praying for God's provision while we were on the phone when the doorbell rang. The "amen" to her prayer was quickly spoken, and I greeted two men at the door, who told me they were here to work on my shelterbelt at no cost. Wow! I was reminded of Isaiah 65:24: *"Before they call I will answer; while they are still speaking I will hear."* The answer was there while we were praying! After that, two more volunteer groups came to help, for which I was grateful.

Getting up and looking out the large picture window, Trevor said, "It looks like there is still a lot of work to be done."

"You are right," I replied, "but I believe there will be a time in the future that the shelterbelt will once again be picture-perfect."

"Will more trees be planted?" Luke asked.

"Yes, Luke, that is the plan."

I am reminded of the story of David. When he was a shepherd, he killed a lion and a bear with his slingshot. Through his faith in the Lord to give him strength, he later killed Goliath with only one stone in his sling. David was given a unique opportunity, but if he had failed to take advantage of that opportunity to build his skill at using his slingshot, he would never have been the Lord's chosen king of Israel.

The Lord has helped me to look at my situations as unique opportunities to minister. While my problems have sometimes been fierce, I have learned to take advantages of those opportunities. The men working in the shelterbelt and the owner of the body shop who repaired the hail damage on my car heard how the great Master Weaver has added vibrant colors of trust to my life.

CHAPTER 19

The Drama Continues

In December 2011, while listening to radio station KJIL, I was reminded to look at the devotional in *The Word for You Today*, published by Celebration, Inc. I felt the challenge to present "The Living Last Supper" again. These words spoke to me:

> Don't allow changing times to change who you are, or make you stop dreaming and give up hope. When your role changes, remember your life is not over. See your own worth as a person, discover your next assignment, gather up your assets, put on your running shoes, and keep on living and giving. No matter how old you are, you can never say you've seen it all. You don't know what God will do with your life before it is over. He has a way of saving the best for last!

For the first time without my coach and valentine by my side, I set out to direct the drama once again, this time at its biggest venue yet, the Beach Schmidt Performing Arts Center at Fort Hays State University in Hays, Kansas. The auditorium provided a fabulous place to present this dynamic ministry on March 24 and 25, 2012. As much as the drama ministered to me, it ministered to the audience and to the men and women who participated.

Rob Scott portrayed Jesus. His response to such an awesome responsibility was amazing. "It is a humbling experience," he said. "I choke up with emotion as I realize how much Jesus loved me as He went willingly to the cross for me. It gives me a glimpse of how much Jesus loved His disciples and the world. I feel humbled and incapable but honored to represent the Savior of the world!"

Toby Scott portrayed the energetic, impetuous Peter. He may not have liked the wig, makeup, or beard, but he felt the drama was a discipleship for the men and knew the camaraderie among the men who had roles in the drama was priceless.

Andrew, portrayed by Shamus Hager, brought his brother Simon Peter to meet Jesus. Shamus felt he was chosen to participate. Andrew was not hesitant to share that "Jesus *is* the King of Kings!"

Dr. Tony Luna portrayed the disciple Simon. He said it was an honor to experience the spiritual transformation of participating in a life-changing experience. He said, "I ask myself how Simon would react to things I do and say. The disciples experienced joy mingled with sorrow. I, as well, experience great joy in presenting the Gospel to an audience who needs to hear the message of Christ's sacrifice for them."

Brad White, who represented Matthew, the tax collector, felt he was privileged to play a disciple and said, "It's important to share with those in attendance that the gospel is for everyone!"

"My belief in myself was very low," Sean Hensley said, "but participating in the powerful ministry of "The Living Last Supper" has made me aware that I am loved and changed by the Resurrected Christ. Even though my past was one of alcohol and drug use, I am now forgiven and am being used to spread the Gospel. Through this ministry I have realized that no sin is too great for the Master to forgive. It is now my turn to pass the exciting news to others. Everyone can be forgiven!"

Scott Tilley felt that James, the Son of Alpheus, was a tremendous fit for him. "I have learned a lot from the portrayal of this disciple," Scott said. "Playing him is an awesome experience, as James has taught me to trade my more obnoxious characteristics for that of being meek and quiet. I am allowed to be bold on one point, as I agree that Jesus *is* the King of Kings!"

"The drama has played a major role in my life, as I can identify with Thomas," said Larry Randall. "It has brought about a definite change. I had been beaten up with life and had made many mistakes. As God revealed Himself to me and spoke to me, my doubt was removed, and I desired to do God's will more than anything else. I am thankful I was obedient and agreed to participate in this electrifying ministry. I have become more aware of the power of God in my life! It has changed my life forever."

The other Judas was represented by Ron Evans. Even though he had an important commitment that could have interfered with his participation, his feeling was that "I am where I need to be." His portrayal was powerful.

"As I have portrayed John the Beloved in the drama," Kelly Torline said, "I have realized we are all pieces of the puzzle in God's plan. As the disciples, we reinforce, reintroduce, and remind the audience of our responsibility to proclaim and spread the good news Jesus came to bring to humankind. The drama has made me realize that, no matter who I am or what I am, God loves me and wants me to be His child."

When Shane Collins accepted the role of James, the Son of Zebedee, he said he felt honored to be involved in a unique and emotionally moving ministry.

Don Dupree, portraying Judas Iscariot, felt his acceptance of the role would reveal to the audience that no one must deny Jesus.

Bartholomew, portrayed by Dan Smith, gave him the knowledge that "I can do something out of my comfort zone" to bless an audience.

Will Ellis, who represented the Servant in the Upper Room, felt the drama produced a "melting together of lives" and that it was a fantastic way to improve his family's relationships and draw them closer to one another.

Mary Magdalene, portrayed by Amanda Lang, gives the audience a vital message, announcing, "He is alive!" after she has seen the resurrected Christ. She is overcome with emotion as she makes the announcement. Amanda's personal feeling was that "it is an awesome honor that has been given to me, as I share the good news with the audience. It has also helped me grow spiritually as I participate in sharing the good news of Christ's resurrection. I know, in my life, *He is alive!*"

Rachel, sister of Micah ben Lazarus, prepared the Passover meal for the disciples and was portrayed by Kyleen Stimpert. Kyleen felt the drama gave her a purpose in life and brought her an abundance of enrichment. "My participation was by divine appointment," she said.

Josh Roesner, portraying Micah ben Lazarus, said, "I have experienced a change in my life, and I am fulfilled!"

Bud Estes, the production manager, said he feels the ministry of "The Living Last Supper" touches many individuals and fulfills Jesus' call for us to spread the Gospel in an effective manner. "I feel it is the most powerful tool available today to spread the good news of salvation," he said.

"I saw the drama with my mother and dad and Luke when it was in Dodge City," Coby said. "I thought it was wonderful, and I was proud of you, Ma, as you were the narrator."

Wistfully, Brady said, "I sure hope I can see it sometime. It sounds awesome."

"Yep! Me, too," Trevor added.

"Living Last Supper" Disciples & Christ freeze

CHAPTER 20

Jesus Is Enough

As the chapters of your great grandma and great grandpa and that of your grandpa have been closed, I know I must keep on living and giving, as my role is not over. Now I enter a new chapter of my own and write my own story. I know it will be exciting and adventurous, and the Master Weaver of my life will continue to show me the way. With Him, my wisdom, power, and strength are unlimited. With confidence and trust, the pot of gold at the end of the rainbow, filled with love, is mine now. My desire is to share that fragrant love with whomever I meet. *Jesus is enough!*

Someday you will graduate from high school, and try your wings. I know life will be a fantastic journey. Thank you for listening to your grandpa's and my story. I remind all of you that your grandpa had fun with you. He took you pheasant hunting and took your dads and you to the hardware store early the day after Thanksgiving to get the best of the bargains.

"I remember we were the first in line because he believed in being early," recalled Earl Ray.

"The best part was coming back to the farm and eating cinnamon rolls," said Trevor.

"We always sat at the table filling out the rebate forms to get the money as soon as possible," laughed Josh.

"He also took us on sleigh rides and hay rack rides," Luke added.

"I remember the year Pa bought pheasants and turned them out of the cage, hoping that seeing them fly would be fun," recalled Coby. "He also hoped that one of our Dads would be able to shoot one."

"Brady, do you have a memory?" I asked.

Brady nodded. "After we opened our gifts, Grandpa always gave each one of us an envelope with some money in it. I was always excited as I waited to see how much money was in my envelope."

"I have another memory I want to mention," Josh said. "I think the best memory I have is us standing around in a circle before we left the farm to go home, and Grandpa praying for us."

"Your memories have been a Christmas present for me. Thanks, guys! And now let's go enjoy some of my homemade cookies."

"Grandma?"

"Yes, Brady?"

"Thanks for sharing your and Grandpa's story." He looked down at his hands.

"What is it, Brady?" I asked.

"Before we enjoy your cookies," he said, "do you have any advice for us?"

That was a tough question, as I wanted my grandsons to have lives as fulfilling as Orlando's and mine had been. After thinking about it for a few moments, God gave me the answer.

My advice to you is to have fun, enjoy life, and seize the moments for splendid memories, but much more important is to follow God's leadership. God will lead you along the path He has designed for you, a path that is uniquely tailor-made just for you! It is important to be radically obedient, as the reward is Heaven as your eternal home.

Difficult circumstances will come in life, but *know* that your life is like a tapestry. When that piece of tapestry is seen from the back, it appears to be threads hopelessly tangled, but when it is seen from the front, when it is finally finished, it is breath-taking because it was woven by the Master Weaver, by loving, nail-scarred hands. Individually, the many-colored threads don't make sense, but when woven together, the result is a harmonious pattern of exquisite beauty.

We can be sure that every detail in our lives of love for God is worked into something good. (Romans 8:28 MSG)

Find a way to be involved in someone else's life. You will be rewarded beyond your wildest dreams. I miss my role as a pastor's wife, but I try to find ladies who need a friend, as many need someone to show them love and compassion. It is a joy to me to find a person who may need a few weeks of discipleship to deepen his or her walk with God. I love being involved with my piano and flute students. Following a spring recital in which all of them have shared their talents, I realize that the teaching relationship doesn't just nurture musical skills—it shapes lives.

Never forget that, just as your grandpa left a Godly heritage, you, too, must not just live for today but set goals for your future and honor God. Then you, too, may leave a Godly heritage for those left behind when you go to your heavenly home.

I love all of you. Remember that, whenever you leave the farm to go home and I am standing in the driveway, waving goodbye. I am saying, "Until we meet again!"

One Year Later

It is Christmas Day 2012. We are gathered as a family around the festive dining room table, and I would like for us to reminisce. Having finished eating our choice of pecan, cherry cheese, or blueberry pie a la mode, I think it would be wonderful to share memories.

Deanna, our oldest daughter, is the first to share a memory: "I learned that being the daughter of a pastor requires keen listening skills. A sermon was more than just a sermon; it was also the basis for a quiz that would inevitably follow on Sunday afternoon. I also learned that a sermon was a time to be quiet. I recall sitting with the youth group on a Sunday morning being noisy, and my daddy would stop preaching, lower his head, and stare at his notes until I was quiet. Needless to say, I was concerned about the repercussions that would come later in the day. My daddy would wait until after lunch to talk with me concerning my disruption in the service, but he did it with care and love. I remember one time when Denise and I were sitting in the back of the sanctuary laughing, and he stopped preaching and told us to come sit in the front pew. Despite these experiences, I learned from my precious daddy's sermons. I was proud that he taught me about Jesus. After I left home, I often thanked him for teaching me eternal truths. Some of his final words to me were, 'Reach out and grasp all that Jesus has for you and never give up. Continue to serve Jesus to the best of your ability, and we will meet in heaven one day.' He was an extremely loving and caring daddy."

Denise, our middle daughter, went next: "I knew the life of a pastor was busy, especially after a worship service. My dad, as the pastor, would make his way around to everyone in his congregation. I remember when I was a teenager, during that busy time, he still made sure I knew I was important. If I needed a few dollars to buy pizza with the youth group, instead of simply opening his wallet, handing me the money, and dismissing me from his presence, he put his arm around me and held me close until the conversation was over. He turned a simple moment into a lasting memory. His final words to me were, 'You have always stood by your husband in ministry, and it has been my delight to see your support. I know growing up in a pastor's home has its ups and downs, but I have tried to be the best example I could be as a dad.' I remember when I was a teenager and I wasn't allowed to do as I desired, I wrote poems to my dad to vent my feelings. He wrote loving and caring poems back to me, reassuring me I was loved, even though I wasn't allowed to do everything I desired. I will also treasure the memory of his taking his grandsons pheasant hunting. My dad passed on to all three of us daughters an amazing, Godly heritage. He was ready to meet his Savior. On Saturday, while he was in tremendous pain, he simply said, 'Daddy to Jesus.'"

Charlene, our youngest, shared too. "After I was born," she said, "I was nicknamed Charlie. Daddy called me that often, as well as 'my little girl.' He loved to hear me play my flute. Before he passed away, he wrote me a note that said, 'Your flute playing has always brought me such joy and delight. A Sunday service is not complete unless I can listen to you using your talent to glorify God. Your flute is more than just an instrument; it is an extension of your heart.' My daddy was a wise steward. I know the cost of flute lessons in Hutchinson, Kansas, were expensive, especially when one considers gas, a meal, purchasing music, and, of course, shopping. During the time he was ill, I was his chauffer to KU Medical Center. Even though it was difficult seeing him suffer, I felt it was a way I could show my love. Once, when Denise and I took him for a radiation treatment in Garden City, Kansas, we asked him about his favorite song. He responded quickly with "Blessed Assurance." We sang the song as we were traveling. That song was his testimony and reminder of his faithful walk with his Savior. I was thrilled that I had the privilege of playing his favorite song at his memorial service. It was difficult, but it was an honor. I recall his being so proud of his deer-hunting skills. He loved sharing the story of hunting a twelve-point buck, and shooting him on the run three hundred yards away. In fact, two of his handsome, treasured deer heads are hanging in the basement of our home. All of us, as his daughters, enjoyed his teasing. We also knew that he was a disciplinarian. It wasn't just about right and wrong but about teaching us what it means to serve our heavenly Father faithfully."

That Christmas Day, as I listened to our daughters talk, it became apparent to me that, even though Orlando was no longer physically with us, the spirit by which he lived continued. Looking at our daughters and our grandchildren, I could see that the threads of the great tapestry of our lives were now a part of their stories too.

As I sat with my family, I thought of Orlando's Bible, and the verses he had highlighted during a lifetime of ministry. Then I thought of the words the Apostle Paul wrote to a young minister named Timothy, verses I could almost hear Orlando reading to us now:

> *I have fought the good fight, I have finished the race, I have kept the faith. Now there is in store for me the crown of righteousness, which the Lord, the righteous Judge, will award to me on that day—and not only to me, but also to all who have longed for His appearing.* (2 Timothy 4:7–8)

CPSIA information can be obtained at www.ICGtesting.com
Printed in the USA
LVOW11s0118080515

437614LV00002B/4/P